CHICAGO PUBLIC LIBRARY
SULZER REGIONAL
4455 N. LINCOLN AVE.

Chicago Collection

Chicago Lincoln Statue, Lincoln Square

The John and Mary Jane Hoellen
Chicago History Collection
Chicago Public Library

R00910 21269

The
Chicago Public Library

REF
NA
2340
.A73
1989
Vol. 7

Call No. R00910 21269

Branch CONRAD SULZER REGIONAL LIBRARY

JAN   1993   Form 178

**Volume 7:
Alternative
Visions**

ARCHITECTURE
CHICAGO

**Chicago Chapter
American
Institute of
Architects**

The information about the projects in this book represents the CCAIA's best efforts to identify the architect for a given project, and is based on information provided by the firm submitting the project for an award. If there are any questions, the submitting firm should be contacted for further clarification.
Cover: First Baptist Church, Columbus, Ohio by Harry Weese and Associates; Photo: Balthazar Korab

Published by:
Chicago Chapter AIA
53 West Jackson
Chicago, Illinois 60604
ISSN 0899-6903
ISBN 0-929862-02-3
©1989, Chicago Chapter AIA

BENEFACTORS

We wish to express our thanks to the following donor to *Architecture Chicago: Volume 7; Alternative Visions*, without whose contributions this annual would not have been possible.

**Sheet Metal Contractors Association;
Chicago, Cook County and Lake Counties Chapter of SMACNA**

TABLE OF CONTENTS

9 **Introduction**

11 **Preservation in Chicago: History in the Unmaking**
Deborah Slaton, AIA

16 **Roots of Middle Western Planning**
Christopher Vernon

21 **Jung, Aalto, and Wood-- Confluences of the Subconscious**
Ben Weese, FAIA

26 **Alternative Visions: Chicago**
Introduction by Edward Keegan and Virginia Kinnucan

56 **Distinguished Building Awards**
Jury Statement by Jane Lucas, CCAIA Executive Director

94 **Interior Architecture Awards**

148 **Interior Architecture: Ten Year Awards**

156 **Divine Detail Awards**

168 **Twenty-Five Year Award**

172 **Distinguished Service Awards**

178 **Young Architect Award**

183 **Chicago Awards**

188 **Acknowledgements**

INTRODUCTION

The 1989 annual continues our tradition of chronicling the activities and achievements of the Chicago architectural community. A valuable historic reference, it presents the current work of Chicago's architects and thought-provoking essays on the state of the city and its environs. Hopefully, the dialogue generated by this effort will continue to fuel the rich diversity of opinion and discussion within the community.

The work, activities and essays presented in this volume represent the efforts of the two thousand members of the Chicago Chapter AIA. This level of enterprise forms the essence of the contribution of the citizen architect to our city and our society. It can only strengthen the fabric of our profession, our life, and our environment.

Steven F. Weiss, AIA
Chicago Chapter AIA President
June, 1989-May, 1990

Preservation in Chicago: History in the Unmaking

Preservation in Chicago is better known for its failures than for its successes: made more famous by what has been lost than by what has been saved. Perhaps the most striking feature of Chicago's long history of preservation controversies has been the pervasive confusion over landmark designation and the subsequent review process.

The Chicago Commission on Historical and Architectural Landmarks is guided by a Landmark Ordinance which, revised through the efforts of local preservation groups, was signed into law in 1985. The Landmark Ordinance defines specific criteria for the designation of an historic property, based on an evaluation of its inherent historical and architectural significance. The efforts of the Commission have been demonstrated by the designation of 87 landmarks–including 15 historic districts–since the original landmark ordinance was passed in 1968.

It has been the practice when designating landmarks in Chicago to identify the "critical features" of an historic property: those elements or spaces which are of primary importance to the character of the structure. The purpose of identifying these features is to recognize that they deserve special consideration for preservation and merit particular attention in design review.

The identification of critical features must not be confused with the practice of "partial designation," whereby only certain pieces of a building are designated as having landmark status. Partial designation is recognized as a way to avoid the responsibilities of landmark designation. This type of designation typically results in partial demolition, or in the creation of a collage of architectural fragments. The designated elements are sometimes applied as facades to new structures, rather than preserved intact as architectural landmarks.

The process of design review has been developed to evaluate modifications or additions to a building after it has been designated a landmark. The purpose of review is not to tie the hands of the building owner. Rather, the review process provides an informed methodology by which the Landmarks Commission can participate in the decision-making process for Chicago's architectural treasures. Design review is based on a number of specific criteria. Briefly, these criteria require that the critical features are preserved, that the least intrusive means of repair are utilized, and

BLOCK 37

Above: McCarthy Building exterior
Photo: Steve Beal, Chicago Landmarks Commission

MCCARTHY BUILDING

that the historical and physical integrity of the landmark are respected.
Its own Landmark Ordinance makes the Commission responsible for the stewardship of the city's historic structures. The difficulties which attend landmark designation and design review are well known in Chicago. The struggle over our landmarks has been documented in the demolition of the Chicago Stock Exchange and the Schiller Theater, and the preservation (to date) of the Reliance Building, among others. Each year is certain to bring new crises over old buildings. Several recent preservation controversies are discussed below.

The McCarthy Building and Block 37

Block 37 in downtown Chicago is bordered by Washington, Randolph, Dearborn, and State Streets, and contains no less than four properties which are listed on the National Register of Historic Places. There are the McCarthy Building (1872), designed by John M. Van Osdel; the Springer Building (1872) designed by Peter B. Wight and remodeled by Adler & Sullivan in 1887; Harry B. Wheelock's Western Methodist Book Concern, completed in 1899; and the 1892 Unity Building, designed by Clinton Warren. Other buildings of historical and architectural significance on the block include the United Artists Theater, the Commonwealth Edison Substation, and the Stop and Shop Building.

The development of this block was formally addressed in 1982, when numerous civic organizations, including the CCAIA, participated in the drafting of the North Loop Guidelines for Conservation and Redevelopment. The guidelines, which initially recommended preservation of many of the historic buildings on Block 37, finally recommended retention of

12

UNION

the McCarthy Building as a compromise. Following these guidelines, the request for proposals for development of the block in 1983 mandated preservation of at least the McCarthy. Preservation of the McCarthy was cited as a key reason for the city's acceptance of a developer's bid for this parcel. During the following year, the City Council designated the McCarthy as a Chicago Landmark.

The September, 1987, only six months after the revised Chicago Landmarks Ordinance was passed into law by the City Council, the Department of Planning requested revision of the North Loop Guidelines and repeal of the McCarthy Building's landmark status. The Commission on Chicago Landmarks did not hold public hearings, and the city did not follow its own established procedure for de-designation of a Chicago landmark.

In less than a month, the requests for revision of the Guidelines and de-designation of the McCarthy were approved and passed as law by the City Council. This action called into question the value and purpose of civic involvement, and whether there is meaningful protection for Chicago landmarks.

Union Station

Union Station is Chicago's only remaining functioning train station. Designed by Graham, Burnham and Company and its successor firm, Graham, Anderson, Probst & White, the station opened in 1925. Its imposing facades and monumental waiting room attest to the importance of the railroad in the development of the city.

The Commission on Chicago Landmarks took the first step in the landmark designation process for Union Station; it determined that the building was eligible to

Above: Union-Station interior, main waiting room
Photo: Bob Thall, Chicago Landmarks Commission

STATION

CHICAGO

become a landmark. However, the Commission later negotiated an agreement entitled "Grant of Preservation and Conservation Easement," under which the developer agreed to donate an easement to the city for no more than five years. This easement covers only portions of the exterior walls and interior spaces. It also prevents all or part of the building from being designated an official Chicago landmark during the term of the easement unless mutually agreed upon, and only if such a designation does not exceed the scope of the easement.

The CCAIA Board of Directors objected to the agreement, which the Board felt set a dangerous precedent for future planning concerning buildings of architectural and historical significance. By negotiating the easement and approving the development plans which are to be carried out under the agreement, the Landmarks Commission has undermined its own review process. In effect, the agreement gives formal city approval to a plan which delays or prevents landmark designation while recognizing the significance of only selected portions of the building.

The Chicago Tribune Building

The Chicago Tribune Building is internationally recognized as a landmark and is one of Chicago's most important historic structures. Designed by Raymond Hood and John Mead Howells in response to the competition of 1922, it is universally identified with the architecture and history of Chicago.

The Tribune Company and the Chicago Landmarks Commission have entered into an agreement which allows the Tribune to dictate the terms under which it will consent to landmark

Above: Chicago Tribune Building exterior
Photo: Bob Thall, Chicago Landmarks Commission

TRIBUNE BUILDING

designation for the building. The agreement also exempts certain features of the building and certain types of work on the building from design review, once again raising the specter of "partial designation". This agreement confuses the designation process and the design review process by seeking to exclude areas of the building from the design review powers and duties of the Commission. The Landmarks Ordinance defines specific criteria for the designation of an historic property based on the evaluation of its historical and architectural significance, not on future modifications or additions to the building. The process of design review has been developed to evaluate these later changes. Under the proposed agreement, the Landmarks Commission has given up its design review powers and negotiated away its responsibilities.

What is the future of preservation in Chicago? The mechanisms for preservation are in place: the Landmark's Ordinance, the Commission, and the designation and review processes. Many wonderful architectural resources endure, but many more are overlooked or threatened by demolition. For the preservation process to be effective, there must be a political will to conserve our architectural heritage. At the present time, there is no real assurance that the landmarks which remain will be protected for future generations.

Deborah Slaton
Chair, CCAIA Historic Resources Committee

The Roots of Middle Western Planning

"**J**ust now, city planning is rapidly rising on the wave of popular enthusiasm. It has taken our cities by storm... Plans are rapidly being made, and the zealous public, gazing upon their depiction of gaily colored parks, wide boulevards, and ornate bridges, is fired with the desire to make all American cities such pleasing pictures as the clever draughtsman has represented on paper."
Jens Jensen (1911)

"**T**he Roots of Middle Western Planning" was the subject of the Chicago Chapter A.I.A. Design Committee panel discussion held at the ArchiCenter on 13 February 1989. Panelists included Sally Chappell, Professor of Art History at DePaul University; Mary Decker, Director of the Metropolitan Planning Council; Donald Kalec, Professor of Interior Architecture at the Art Institute of Chicago and formerly Curator at the Frank Lloyd Wright Home and Studio; and Christopher Vernon, a landscape architect and doctoral candidate in historical geography at the University of Illinois at Urbana-Champaign.

"**R**egionalist" is not a label commonly applied to Daniel Hudson Burnham. In response to those who might think such a label a misnomer, Sally Chappell opened the discussion with a search for what she termed Burnham's "hidden" regionalism. Chappell suggested that Burnham's attitude toward regionalism might best be described as "bivalent": a synthesis of "regionalism" and "cosmopolitanism." Central to the discussion was Chappell's belief that Burnham was sensitive to and responded to the subtle beauties of the native landscape of the Chicago region, "the limitlessness of the prairie" and "the vast stretches of the inland sea of Lake Michigan." In regard to Burnham's response to the Middle Western landscape, Chappell cited the examples of the World's Columbian Exposition of 1893 and the 1909 Plan of Chicago. Chappell acknowledged that, upon first impression, the plans seem to only reflect familiar, classical European qualities; however, she then called attention to the frequently overlooked informal elements of these plans. Despite the classical nature of the Columbian exposition's Court of Honor, it was the informal elements, such as the naturalistic parklands and the "Wooded Isle" (designed by landscape architects Frederick Law Olmsted, Sr., and Henry Sargent Codman) that

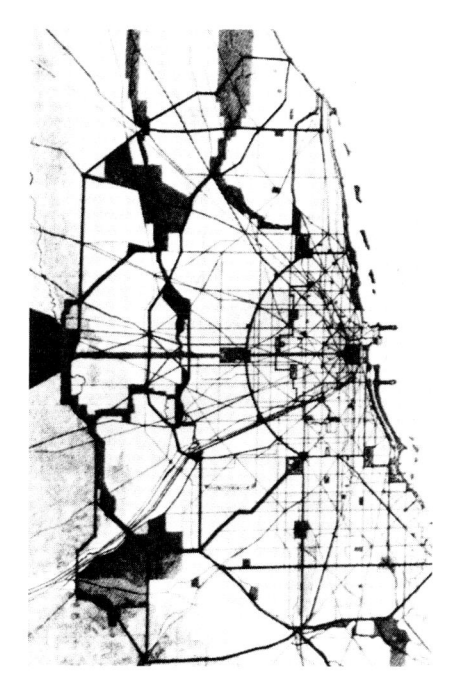

Above: From *The Plan of Chicago*, edited by Charles H. Moore (Chicago: Commercial Club, 1909), Edward H. Bennett and Daniel H. Burnham, architects

dominated the atmosphere of the Exposition. Chappell added that the Court of Honor was only the "counterpoint," not the actual "point" of the exposition.

Informal elements were also employed in the Plan of Chicago. This was reflected in the incorporation of parklands of naturalistic design, both extant (many of which were the work of William LeBaron Jenny) and proposed, and in a forest preserve system (initiated earlier, primarily by Dwight Perkins and Jens Jensen) which "followed the lines of the prairie rivers along the plains." Chappell, in conclusion, stressed that "when we look at the streets and the buildings that came out of Burnham's planning office, we get a cosmopolitan picture; but, when we look at the land, the planning of the green spaces, and the parks and forest preserves, other qualities begin to emerge."

Building upon the themes of regionalism and the significance of the Middle Western landscape, Christopher Vernon elaborated on the planning activities of Walter Burley Griffin and Jens Jensen. Griffin's works which related to city and community planning predate his well-known winning entry in the Canberra competition of 1912. Vernon traced Griffin's interest in the design and planning of exterior spaces back to Griffin's own education in landscape gardening at the University of Illinois at Urbana-Champaign and his later experiences as Wright's landscape architect at the Oak Park studio. Vernon demonstrated how, in general, the scope and scale of Griffin's landscape designs and planning grew progressively larger through time: he began with Griffin's designs for the William Martin residence in Oak Park, Illinois (c. 1903), followed by the Northern Illinois State Normal School campus at Dekalb, Illinois (1906), and then the Millikin Place community at Decatur, Illinois (1910). Vernon characterized Griffin's planned communities as being inwardly-focused enclaves. Griffin typically established "architectonic" relationships, at varying scales, between his built environments and the surrounding landscape. Jensen, although commonly remembered only for his landscape designs, also involved himself in city planning activities. Vernon then outlined Jensen's role in the creation of the Cook County forest

JENSEN

preserve system and Jensen's 1919 plan for "A Greater West Park System," and his 1922 plan for a network of Illinois state parks. Vernon emphasized that "a deep sensitivity to and appreciation of the distinctive prairie landscape of the Middle West" was the primary common bond between Griffin and Jensen. Indicative of their appreciation of the landscape were the "Saturday Afternoon Walks" during which Griffin and Jensen led Chicagoans to remaining natural areas in the city's surrounds. Vernon concluded his discussion by suggesting that this sense of appreciation for the landscape was perhaps heightened by the fact that both Griffin and Jensen witnessed the destruction of many of the last remnants of Chicago's primeval landscape at the hands of urban development and "suburbanization."

Donald Kalec detailed what might be considered Frank Lloyd Wright's design response to the threat of unplanned urban development and suburbanization: Broadacre City. Even though "we think about Wright's Broadacre City occurring sometime in the mid-thirties," Kalec pointed out that Broadacre City may have had its origins as early as 1901. In February of 1901, the *Ladies' Home Journal* published Wright's "quadruple block" plan, in which he grouped four of his prairie houses to enclose a central plot. Wright further developed his quadruple block plan and submitted it as a "non-competitive" entry in the City Club of Chicago's 1913 planning competition for the design of "a typical quarter section of land in the outskirts of Chicago" (Griffin and Jensen also submitted designs). Growing out of Wright's dissatisfaction with the "typical city," Broadacre City *per se* had its genesis in Wright's 1932 book, *The Disappearing City*. In this book, Wright "outlined all of his ideas about what the city should be". Wright continued to develop

Above: A prairie drive and canal were the primary features of Jens Jensen's plan for Chicago (from *A Greater West Park System*).

GRIFFEN

18

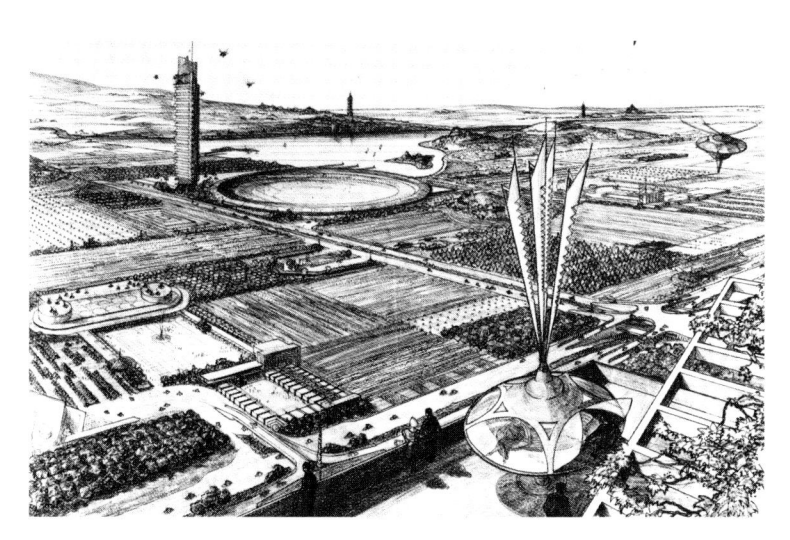

Above: Scene from Frank Lloyd Wright's Broadacre City. ©1958 The Frank Lloyd Wright Foundation

his ideas about Broadacre City in subsequent publications.

Kalec then reviewed the concepts central to Wright's Broadacre City ideals. In contrast to "simply redoing" extant cities, Kalec reported that Wright idealistically sought to decentralize the nation: "to make a continuum across the U.S.A., neither urban nor rural, a little of both, seamless in a way." In what Kalec described as Wright's "most striking proposal," every citizen was entitled to a minimum of one acre of land. Broadacre City, Kalec cautioned, "is more of a philosophical comment about city planning than it is an actual concrete example." Kalec continued that Wright, however, "realized that in order to sell his ideas and philosophy, he needed something physical for people to look at." Wright then directed his newly-created Taliesin Fellowship in the construction of a large-scale model, "representing four square miles of what he thought a holistic, generic section of Broadacre City would look like." Following a review of the design elements of Broadacre City, Kalec continued with a discussion of its impact. Citing that Broadacre City "wasn't a model that was easily graspable, and would have required a social revolution, in a way, to bring it about," Kalec surmised that the impact of Wright's idealized nation was minimal. Broadacre City, Kalec concluded, represented Wright's "way to make a better life for people," and was a "blend of urban and rural, keeping the better of each."

"Why do some plans go from drawings on paper and others do not?" Mary Decker posed and answered this question through an examination of the historical effort to implement Burnham's and Bennett's *Plan of Chicago*. Decker explained that the plan was an integral component of "being in Chicago" and of "the attitudes of the city government, the park district, and the engineers, architects, and

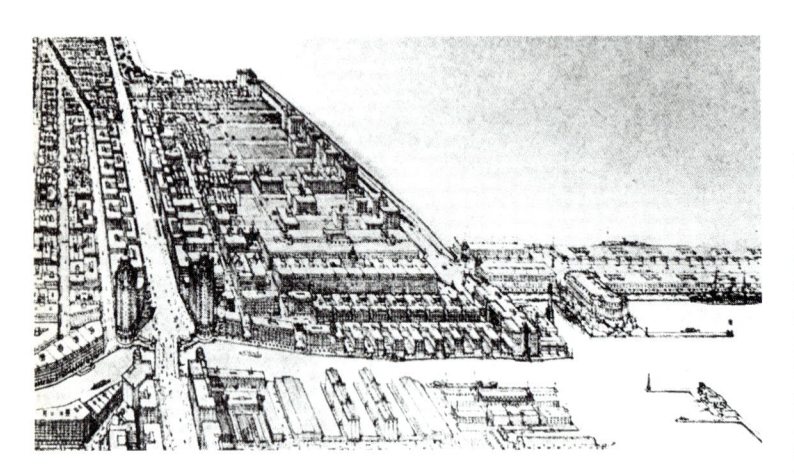

Above: Scene from *Wacker's Manual of the Plan of Chicago*

planners working in the city at that time." Decker continued that the *Plan of Chicago* "became the way of responding to any planning question," and "had an effect on everything that happened in the city over the following decades." What made the 1909 *Plan of Chicago* so remarkable and so powerful? Decker felt that "it has something to do with the acceptance of the plan as distinguished from the adoption of the plan." Public participation in civic improvement, via referenda, and the introduction of the 1913 *Wacker's Manual of the Plan of Chicago* into Chicago public school eighth-grade civics classes were the two primary reasons cited by Decker for the public acceptance of the plan. In her review of the organization and contents of the *Wacker Manual*, Decker emphasized that the manual addressed such non-technical issues as "civic vision" and "competition with other cities." In addition, the manual included what Decker termed "non-market" issues, such as the development of parklands, in which profit was not a motive. Decker emphasized that the eighth-grade students who had used the book in turn conveyed its contents to their parents. For the eighth-grade was generally "as far as anyone went in 1909." Decker stated that implementation of a plan frequently hinges upon public awareness and acceptance of the plan: "it was thought that over one-half of Chicago's population comprehended the contents of the *Plan of Chicago*." Decker concluded that this "could not be said of contemporary plans."

Christopher Vernon

Jung, Aalto, and Grant Wood—Confluences of the Subconscious

"True art is creation, and creation is beyond all theories... Not theories but your own creative individuality alone must decide.
"The unsatisfied yearning of the artist reaches back to the primordial image in the unconscious which is best fitted to compensate the inadequacy and one-sidedness of the present."
C.J. Jung

"Architectural design operates with innumerable elements that eternally stand in opposition to each other. They are social, human, economic, and technical demands that unite to become psychological problems... All this becomes a maze that cannot be sorted out in a rational or mechanical manner... In such cases I work totally on instinct... After I have developed a feel for the program and its innumerable demands have been engraved on my subconscious, I begin to draw in the manner of abstract art. Led only by my instincts I draw... I would like to add that architecture and its details are connected in a way with biology. They are perhaps like large salmon or trout. They are not born mature. They are not even born in the sea or a body of water where they will normally live. They are born many hundreds of miles from their proper living environment."
Alvar Aalto from
"The Trout and the Stream"

Jung and Aalto assert that artistic creativity is an intuitive process, not a rational one. But in our word- and image-dominated culture, we have lost contact with this intuitive process and merely manipulate the end product: words and images. Rational analysis crowds out intuitive synthesis. Jung's insight means that the creative act stands apart from rational analysis or theories. Furthermore, the source of creation is the collective unconscious, with its archetypes and vast substrate underlying our conscious existence. With Jung, consciousness is only a fragment of this vast accumulated archaic resource and must mediate with it to allow its creative release. Aalto goes to the instinctive level to grapple with the whole. So each, in his own way, points to an unconscious stream of stored experiences as the source, carefully nursed to consciousness in the creative act. Aalto cryptically concludes his essay: "We cannot place archaic art lower in our scale of values," a statement strangely congruent with Jung's concepts of archetypes and the collective unconscious. Nowadays, our hectic and dominating rational consciousness continually thwarts this transforming and inexhaustible unconscious resource as it wells up.

In reaching out to the subconscious, we use words like humanistic and organic. But such labels and their meanings are fuzzy and distracting. We often start by naming things before we even see them. Once we see them, the naming becomes less important. Chris Alexander, in his excellent thesis, contrasts the self-conscious with the unself conscious design process—a helpful and analogous insight. Aalto includes Gunnar Asplund as a fellow sojourner by concluding in his poignant eulogy that Asplund honored "the study of psychological problems, 'the unknown human' in his totality."

I rest my case on the hope that the creative act can be spared the preemptive strikes of the interpreters, and with some conviction that creation precedes, and indeed takes precedence, in all modesty, over interpretations and theory.

If one "designs" what happens? With eyes closed, one "lives" oneself into a situation by prowling through all sorts of indirections and daydreams. Without pencil, paper, or words, the best position is supine, meditative, lying on one's back, eyes shut, using the internal eye, walking through, visualizing the unfolding of three-dimensional space in one's head and eventually, with many repeated efforts, light and space first, then descending through detail, color, and texture, seeing everything down to the minutiae. This is not an intellectual process. It is informed by the intellect indirectly, but it is essentially an internalized, intuitive visual process–perceiving in the intuitive rather than the logocentric side of the brain. It is a process which transforms all sources of information, and does not merely relay data. It is also a process that we have moved away from. It should have precedence. It is fresh. It is the source. Graphics and words are subservient to it. Nowadays, we start with graphics and words as ends. But they stand in opposition to it. They are propaganda. They should only be means.

I have indicated with help from Jung and Aalto that designing forms is a complex, internalized, intuitive, neurological process. If this is a viable explanation, which I believe it is, how and where does it thrive? This is where the idea of regionalized and localized comes in. I suggest it flourishes better in a contained, concentrated, localized, defined, limited, geographical arena. Before we discuss this as a process taking place at some specific locale, we must first dismiss regionalism as a style. To define regionalism as a style leads to trouble and endless argument. Architects should leave the identification and definition of regionalism to the historians and history. If a regional style is projected into the present, it is belittled, outshown, and considered dated, ethnically quaint, nuts and berries. It is defenseless and overshadowed by today's sophisticated global outlook, by mass-marketing methods, the broad reach of technology, and by so-called "world-class" architects descending on every region. We cannot defend the idea of regionalism as a style. But we can defend a regionalized process, the process of concentrating in a restricted area and scope, as a viable method to plumb those depths. Restricted geography and focus allows for immersion in the region. It creates the potential not for a broader but for a deeper experience. In the past, restricted movement was a fact, producing distinctive regional architecture. More recently, we can name architects whose movements were restricted–by accident or choice–intensifying the process of their design search. I have already mentioned Aalto and Asplund. They traveled, but they were geographically rooted in their outlook. Asplund built only in Sweden. Mackintosh was also very connected to his environment. He never got to Vienna, though Josef Hoffman implored him to come. Voysey never even visited the continent, instead concentrating on the Lake District specifically. These are a few examples to suggest that rootedness and concentration on a limited plane, neither distracted nor deflected, opens the possibilities of probing deeply with fresh insights and fresh form. Another correlating phenomenon of these architects mentioned is that their works were modest both in size and in number–some twenty, thirty, or forty buildings at most over a lifetime. The disciplined restriction of scope affords time and freedom to mine the resources at hand, the eye quietly seeing and the intuition responding. This is the description not of a style, but of a method, a way of looking at what is before your eyes. This leads us to the story of Grant Wood. He is regional. He is famous. And he presents a link between art and architecture through his powers of visualization. His story helps illuminate the creative path, but also illustrates the pitfalls along the way as well. Grant Wood, artist and protagonist, championed and popularized the term "regionalism." He makes an interesting study of what I can now describe as a regionalized method. Wood was born in northeast Iowa near Anamosa in 1891 and moved off the farm to Cedar Rapids in 1901. A key fact is that he had no academic training, but was essentially self-taught. Throughout his life, he remained suspicious of the academy and its painters, although he did acknowledge his debt to the arts and crafts school he attended briefly in Minneapolis.

Above: *Stone City, Iowa* by Grant Wood; oil on wood panel, 1930.
Collection, Joslyn Art Museum, Omaha, Nebraska
Gift of Art Institute of Omaha, 1931
Photo: © Josyln Art Museum

GRANT

Above: *The Birthplace of Herbert Hoover*, by Grant Wood; oil on masonite, 1931. Purchased jointly by the Des Moines Art Center and the Minneapolis Institute of Art. The purchase was made possible through an exchange of gifts made by Mrs. Howard Frank of Oskaloosa and the Des Moines Association of Fine Arts, 1982.

He later worked in Chicago as a silversmith at the Kalo shops and attended night school at the Art Institute. He traveled abroad to Paris and Italy with his painter friend Marvin Cone, painting Impressionistic details of doorways and churchyards. But his art was hermetic, uninfluenced by any of the current continental movements. Cone finally said to him, "We don't belong here; let's go back home," where in Cedar Rapids in the late twenties, his mature subject matter and expression came to him as he says, literally, "in his own back yard."

Between 1930 and his death in early 1942, he produced his stylistically unique work and championed a regional movement. This period produced only thirty easel paintings. Note the similarly limited work product of the architects mentioned earlier. Over an eleven-year period, the addition of two murals, lithographs and sketches did not expand his output significantly. If he had painted American Gothic (1930) alone, he would still remain important. Stone City (1930) is probably his second most famous work. He founded a movement that encouraged other regionalists, chiefly John Steuart Curry and Thomas Hart Benton, to reclaim their midwestern roots and emphasize the social, political and economic atmosphere of the times–the robust family life and basic homegrown American values pitted against the deep depression, dust bowl and loss of identity. With his ever-widening success, Wood drew national attention. He was drawn into the diversions of the national lecture circuit, high society, honorary degrees and polemic. This diversion slowed his work product to a trickle. Of the thirty paintings he produced between 1930 and 1942, twenty-four were completed before 1936. As propaganda spokesman for "nationalized regionalism," he had subverted his own precious backyard discovery

and his idea of rootedness.
The myth of Hercules and Antaeus was reenacted in the story of Grant Wood. Antaeus, the progeny of Earth Mother, remained invincible through constant nurturing contact with his life source, but is finally destroyed by Hercules, who plucks him on high and strangles him in the alien air. Likewise, separated from his source, Grant Wood virtually ceased creating and wasted himself instead in controversy. Regionalized expression is self-limiting. It renews and grows through continual confrontation with the specific, which is an end in itself.
In Wood's case, by overstressing socio-economic symptoms in depression America, critics miss the key link of perception and place that confirms his regionalized expression. To link perception and place, **we** must see as Wood saw: the multiple vanishing points and light sources, the possible meanings or origins of the strange organic forms, or the technical application of paint that produces them. His pregnant, billowing forms, bursting from within with a powerful natural force, are a direct translation into paint strokes of a lifetime of stored images. Many have painted bucolic scenes, but his are indelible. His singular perceptions are the essence of a regionalized expression– images floating before him awake or dreaming, directly and freshly translated into form. He saw as no one else saw. Was he not revealing to us the collective unconscious?
As Grant Wood and his circle moved away from their source, their creative strength diminished, and so ends the story of Grant Wood.
There are many parallel streams of evidence leading to confluences, uniting such diverse people as Aalto and Jung, as each in his own way consciously acknowledged collective, unconscious sources. Grant Wood also tapped these sources, but understood them less well. When he lost contact with them, his creative activity virtually ended. There are many parallel streams; I have mentioned only a few. What is covered here are only my impressions. They are not a set of rules. They are not absolute, nor in any sense do they deserve the label of architectural or art theory.

Ben Weese, FAIA
Weese Hickey Weese
Architects, Ltd.

W O O D

CHICAGO: ALTERNATIVE VISIONS

"**Y**oung architects are invited to submit a solution for a building, planning concept, ornamental detail, or landscaping idea which portrays an anticipated or unforeseen change in Chicago's condition, whether it be economic, political, social, technological, or ecological. **T**he exhibition is open to all architects, thirty-five years of age or younger, who live or work in Illinois within forty miles of Chicago. An architectural license is not required. **T**he public at large will be asked to vote by ballot to select the winning solutions. Prizes will be awarded according to majority vote."
–from the *Alternative Visions: Chicago* call for entries.

"**C**hicago is destined to become the center of the modern world, if the opportunities in her reach are intelligently realized, and if the city can receive a sufficient supply of trained and enlightened citizens."
–Walter D. Moody, 1911
Wacker's Manual of The Plan of Chicago

Shifting trends of architectural fancy, economic cycles of boom and bust, and changing political administrations impact the overall shape of cities; only a few outstanding visions have had the power to shape the physical form of the city in the long term. *Alternative Visions: Chicago* builds on a tradition of speculative proposals by architects for altering the form of the city and our perceptions of it.

Incorporated in 1837 and almost entirely rebuilt following the Great Fire of 1871, Chicago is one of the world's youngest major cities. Since its inception, Chicago's physical form has been dominated by the surveyor's grid, a rigid organization which allowed for vast development in a short span of time. Several plans for the city proposed major interventions in this overall structure. Early plans for parks and lakefront established a pattern for private initiative and involvement shaping public policy which still enriches the city today. Daniel Burnham and Edward Bennett's Plan of Chicago, a private venture, was handed down in the form of a textbook to generations of Chicago schoolchildren. Part of a curriculum in municipal economy, the book discussed the plan in social, economic, and architectural terms, making "the child feel that in him rests the responsibility of assisting Chicago to attain her future greatness."

Walter D. Moody's aspirations for Chicago remain only partially realized. *Alternative Visions: Chicago* reflects his conviction that individual citizens must share in the inherited knowledge of the making of cities and that these citizens must be actively engaged in the intelligent and responsible use of this knowledge to help create a vibrant and active city.

Alternative Visions: Chicago exhibits speculative views of those architects who will be responsible for designing Chicago in the twenty-first century. Entries explore a variety of issues now facing the city: development of the lakefront and parks, the future of public housing, housing options for the homeless, innovative public transportation systems, symbols for Chicago, and the role of the architect in society. More whimsical solutions depict Chicago as a subtropical city and as a Venice-like locale where canals and gondolas replace streets and cars. In presenting these ideas about the city and it future potential, these young architects hope to foster a dialogue with the public about the city we all share.

**Edward Keegan
Virginia Kinnucan**
1989 CCAIA Young
Architects Committee

ALTERNATIVE VISIONS:

CHICAGO

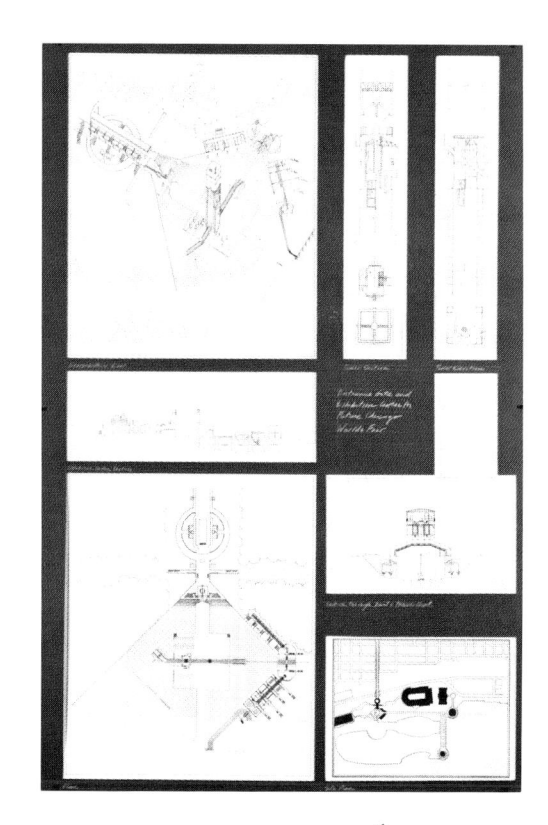

▶
Entrance Gate and Exhibition Centers for a Future World's Fair on Chicago's Lakefront
Michael J. Abraham

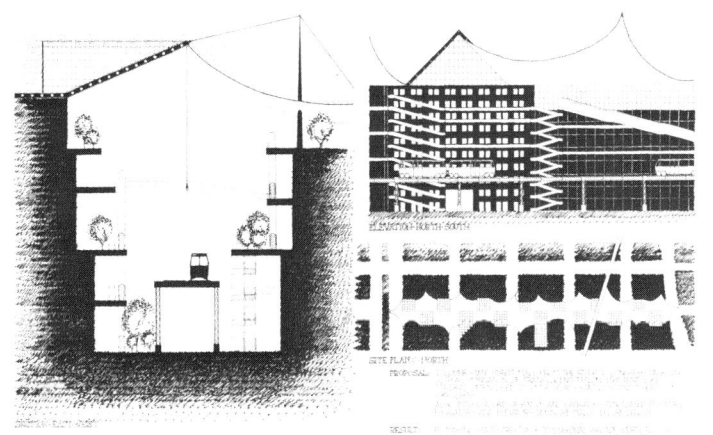

◀
The "New and Improved" State Street Mall
Alan J. Armbrust

CHICAGO: ALTERNATIVE VISIONS

◀ **Chicago Color Vision**
Christian W. Blaser

▶ **The Renovation of Navy Pier**
Richard Carr

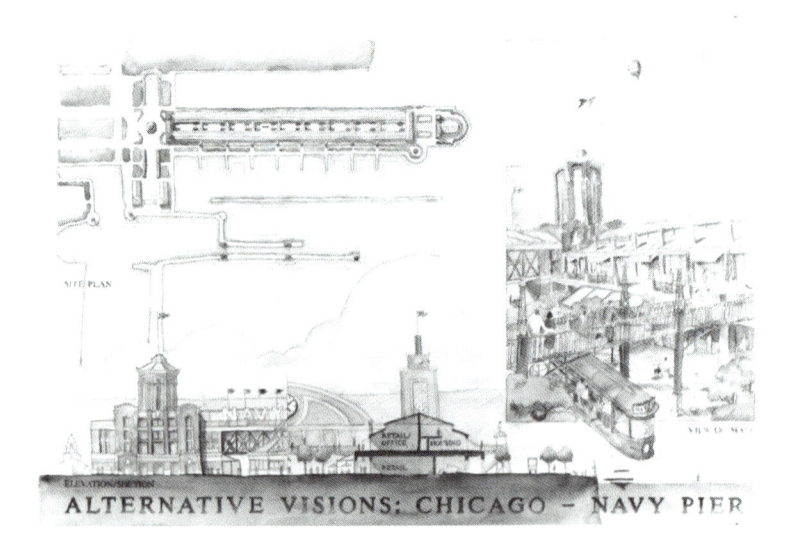

ALTERNATIVE VISIONS:

CHICAGO

▼
To In.hab'it (inhabit) the Line
Craig T. Cernek

▲
WE - in turning of 2000
Chun L. Cham

CHICAGO: ALTERNATIVE VISIONS

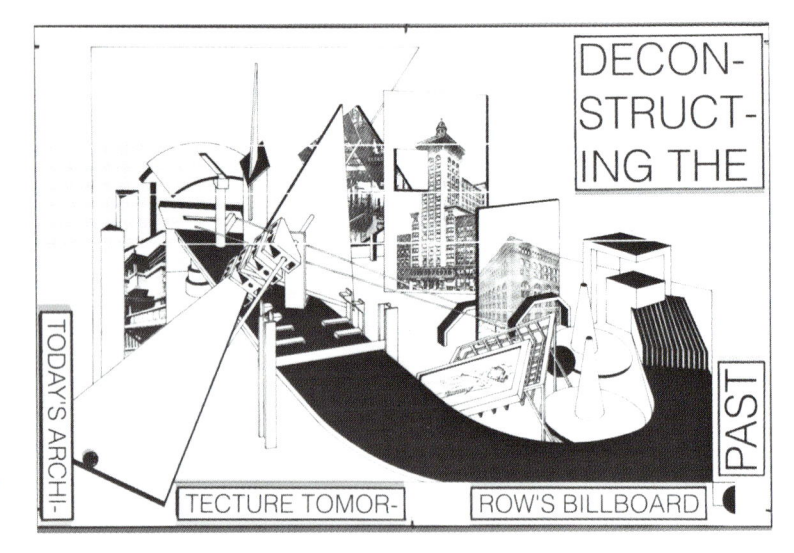

Deconstructing the Past
John E. Dancer

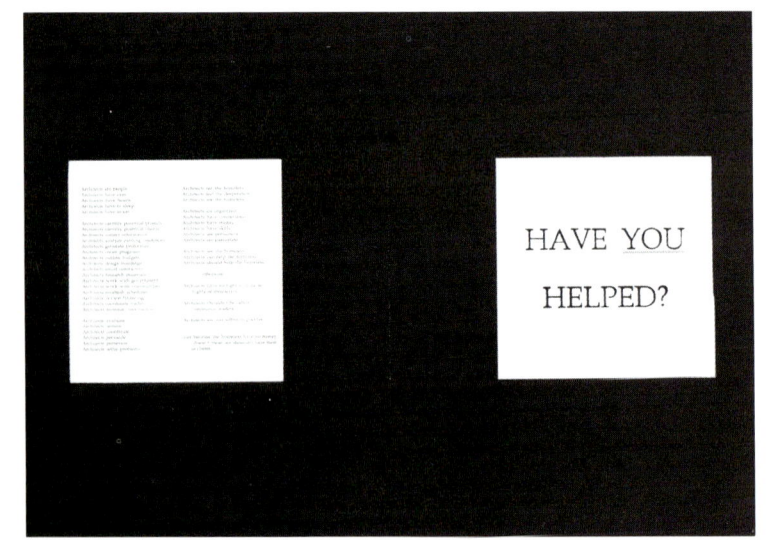

Architects
Eric Emmett Davis

ALTERNATIVE VISIONS:

CHICAGO

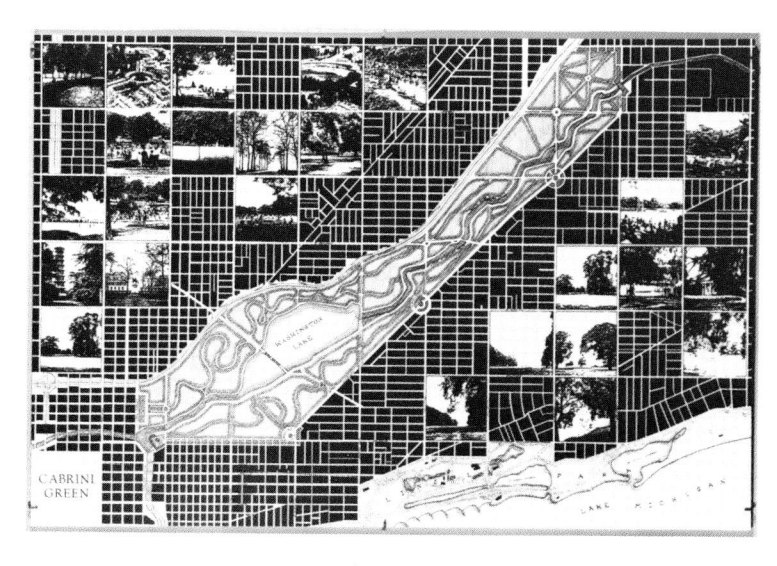

◄
Cabrini Green
Gregory J. DeStefano

▶
21st Century Library
Richard S. Drinkwater

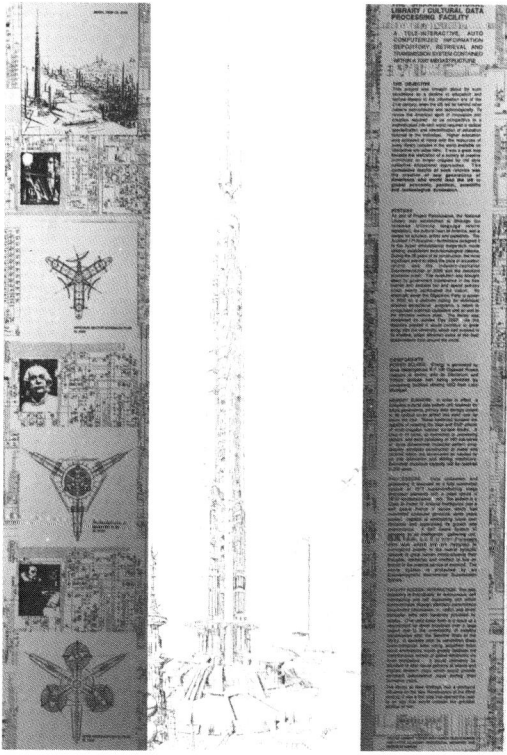

31

CHICAGO: ALTERNATIVE VISIONS

▶
Loop 2001
Maura Feaheny

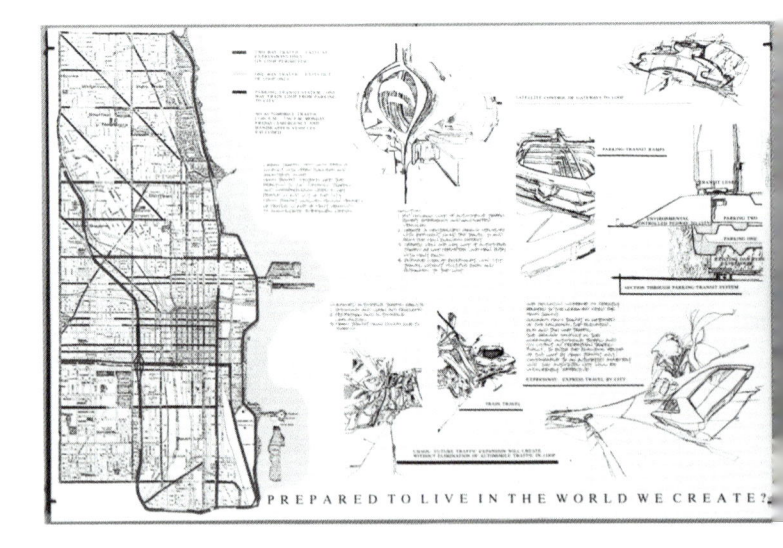

◀
Transgression
Thomas V. Economou

32

ALTERNATIVE VISIONS: CHICAGO

▶
On the Boulevard
Charles W. Fill

◀
View Looking North
Paul Froncek

CHICAGO: ALTERNATIVE VISIONS

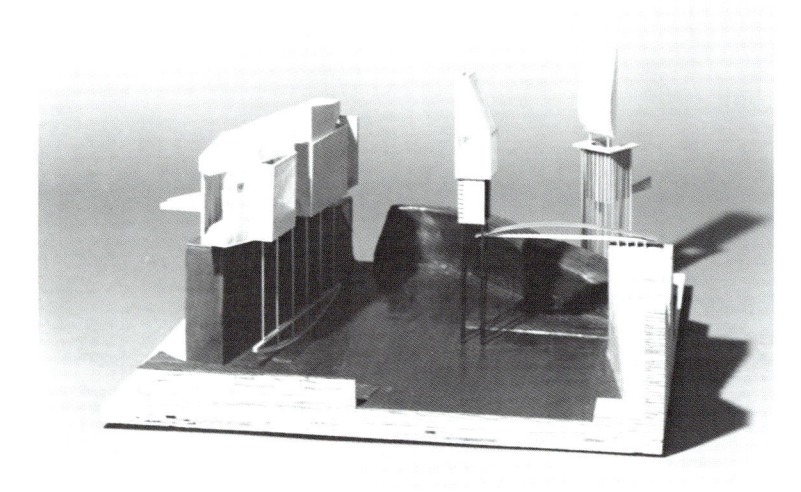

▶
**Object Sanctuary:
Visitor Inhabitant**
Douglas A. Garopolo

◀
**The Baths of
Schaumburg**
Gilbert Gorski

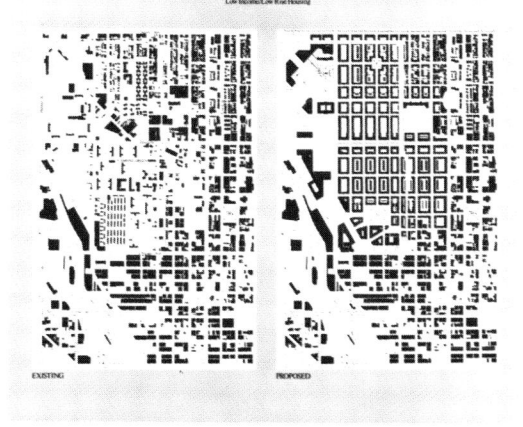

ALTERNATIVE VISIONS: CHICAGO

ALTERNATIVE VISIONS:
CHICAGO

CABRINI GREEN
Low Income/Low Rise Housing

EXISTING   PROPOSED

◄
Cabrini Green: Low Income/Low Rise Housing
Darrell B. Griest

▶
A Gateway to the Arts
Gabriel Guemes

35

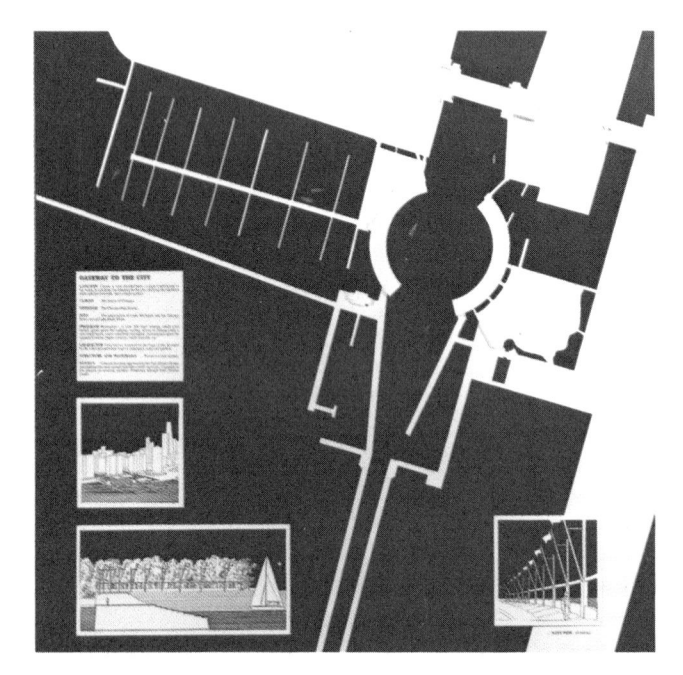

CHICAGO: ALTERNATIVE VISIONS

A Gateway to the City
Miriam Gusevich

The Plan of Chicago: An Urban Design for Tomorrow
Mark Hinchman

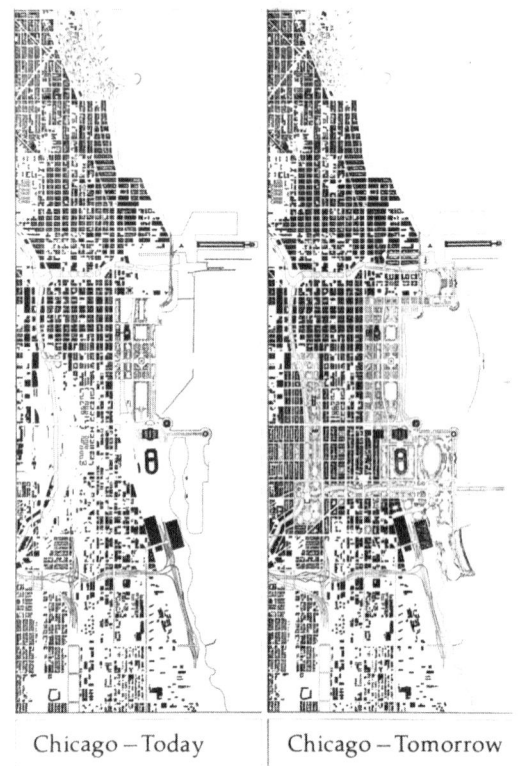

Chicago – Today

Chicago – Tomorrow

36

ALTERNATIVE VISIONS: CHICAGO

▶
**Chicago in 2002—
A "Tropical" Winter
Day**
Dean Huspen

◀
**The City
Re-assembled**
Timothy J. Jachna

CHICAGO: ALTERNATIVE VISIONS

▼
Theoretical Considerations of the Single-family Dwelling
Bill Joslin

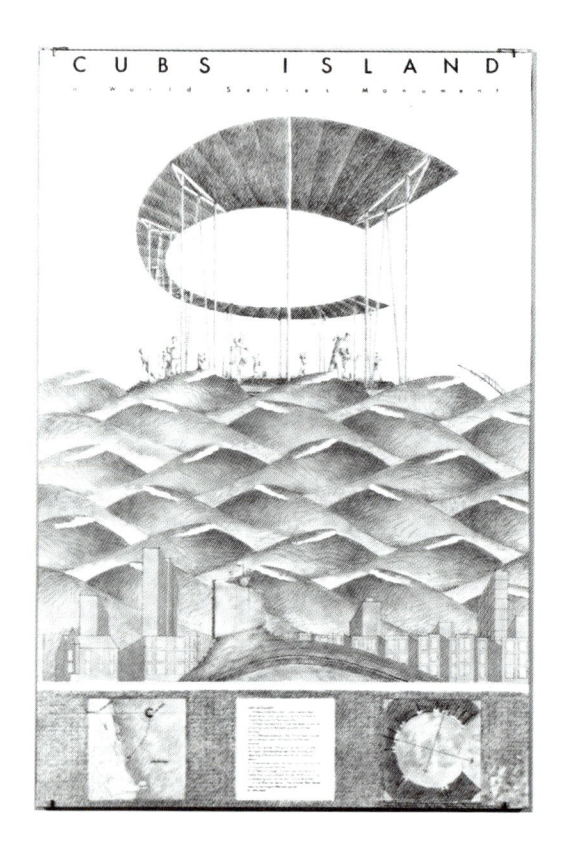

▲
Cubs Island - A World Series Monument
David Jennerjahn

ALTERNATIVE VISIONS: CHICAGO

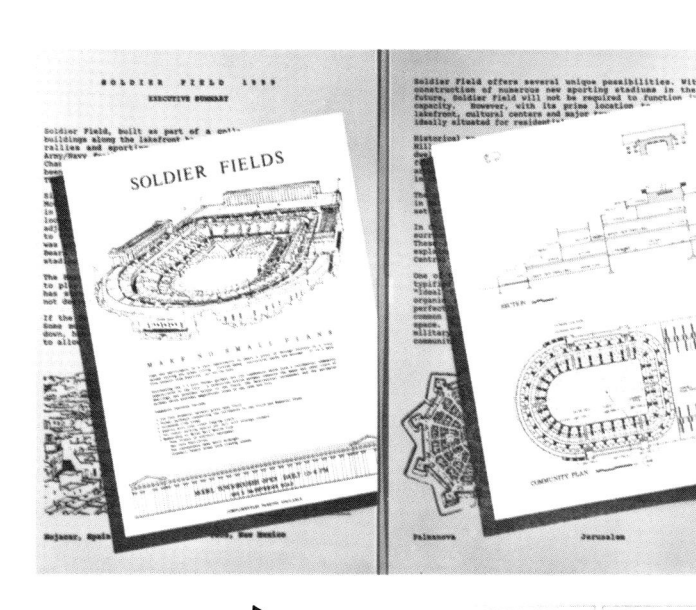

◀
Soldier Fields
Nathan Kipnis

▶
Whither Chicago?
Paul Krieger

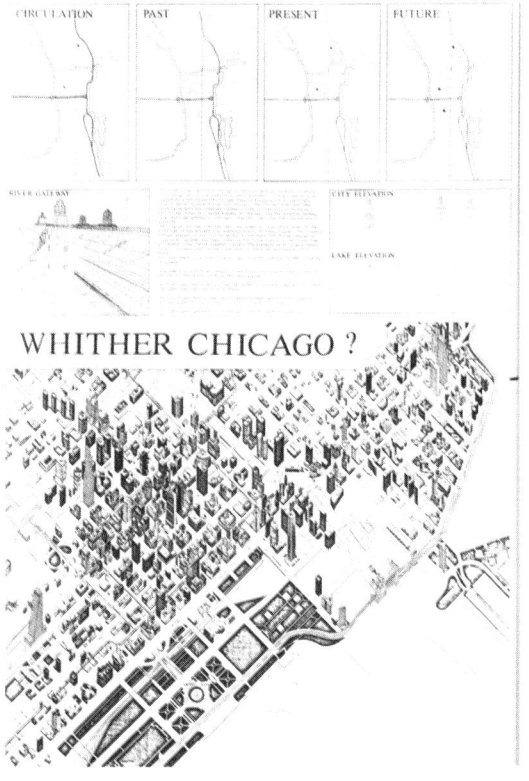

39

CHICAGO: ALTERNATIVE VISIONS

▶
Third Place

Maritime Center - Chicago
Joseph E. Lambke

◀
Communities within a Megastructure: Twin Megaframes, carrying factory-finished residences, joined to form common space in between
Colby Lewis

ALTERNATIVE VISIONS:

CHICAGO

◀
**Freeway Expression:
A Point of
Orientation**
Michael F. Logue

▶
Politicus Satiricus
Peter Madimenos

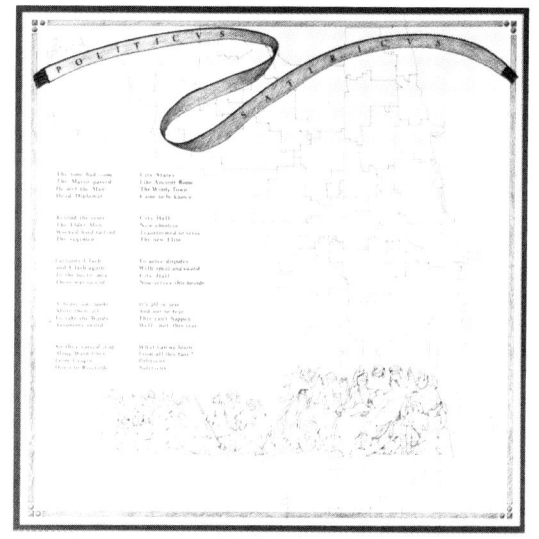

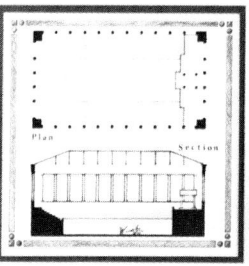

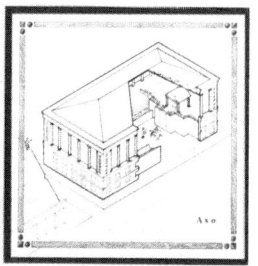

CHICAGO: ALTERNATIVE VISIONS

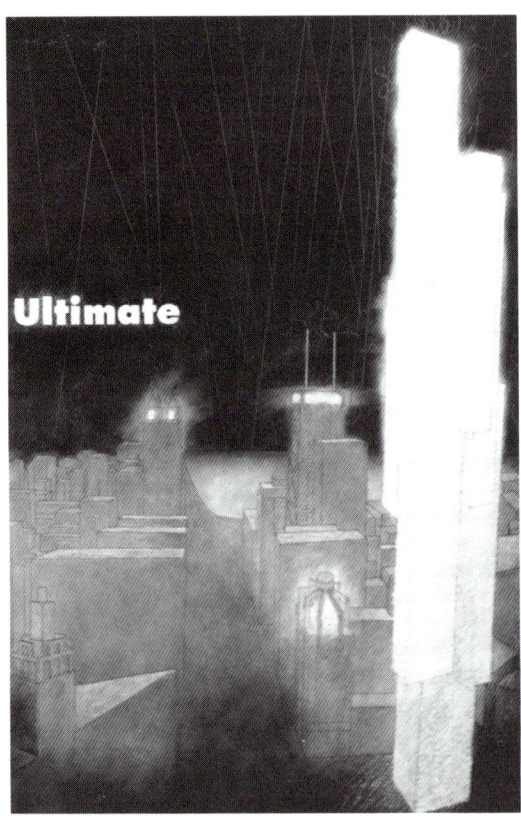

◀
**Ultimate
Skyscraper -
Chicago**
Randall Mattheis

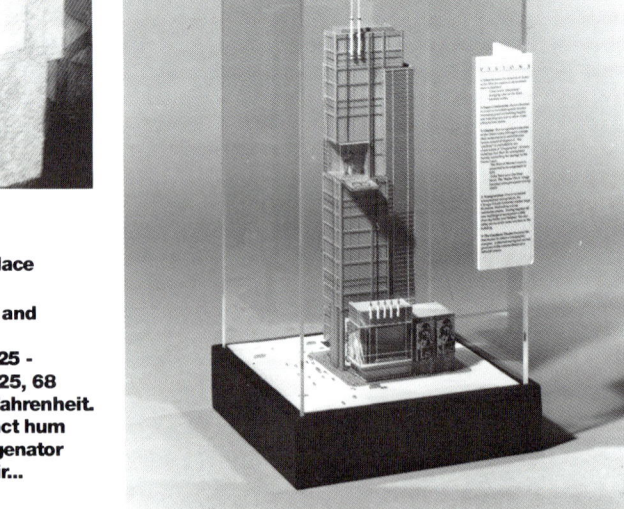

▶
Second Place

**Dearborn and
Randolph
02/25/2025 -
February 25, 68
degrees Fahrenheit.
The distinct hum
of an oxygenator
fills the air...**
Dan Meis

ALTERNATIVE VISIONS:

CHICAGO

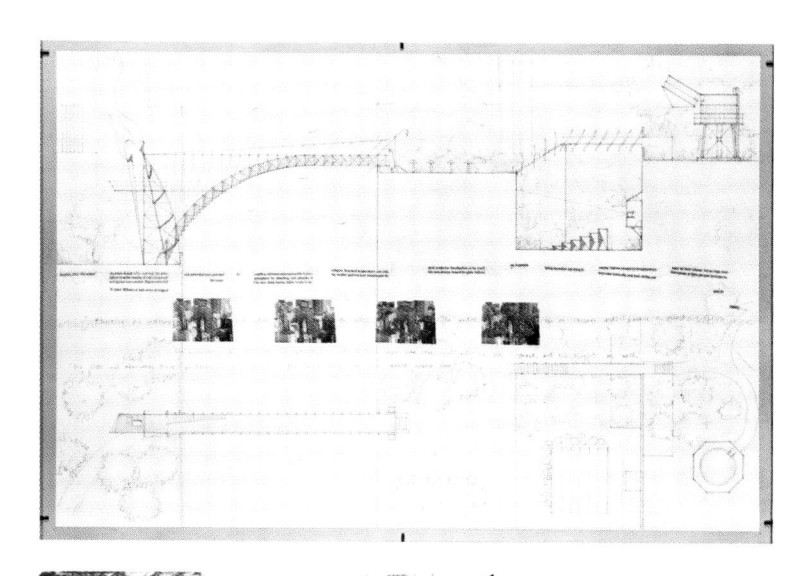

▶
Roof Forest
Kimberli Meyer

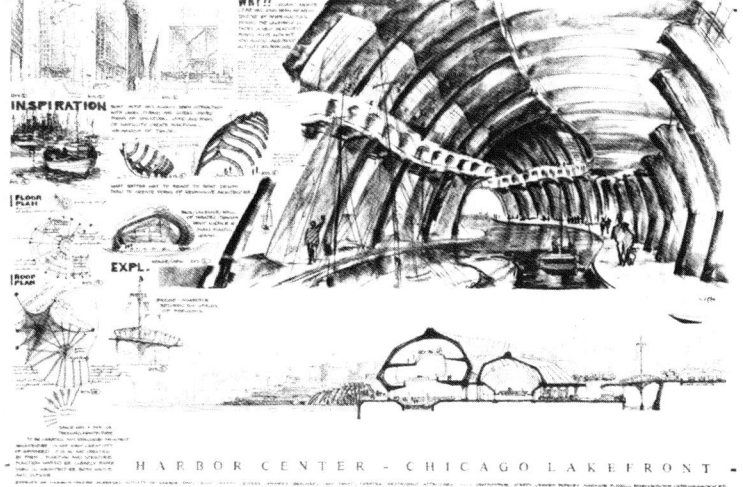

◀ **Harbor Center**
Wieslaw Piotr Moskal

43

CHICAGO: ALTERNATIVE VISIONS

▼
**Paradigm or Pariah?
-An Architectural
Intervention into
Daniel Hudson
Burnham's Timeless
Plan for Chicago**
Paul Stephen Pettigrew

▲
**Energy Efficient
High-Rise
Prototype 3A**
Robert J. Piotrowski

ALTERNATIVE VISIONS: CHICAGO

◀
World's Columbian Exposition Centennial, Grant Park
Thomas N. Rajkovich

▶
An Island in the Lake
Robin R. Randall

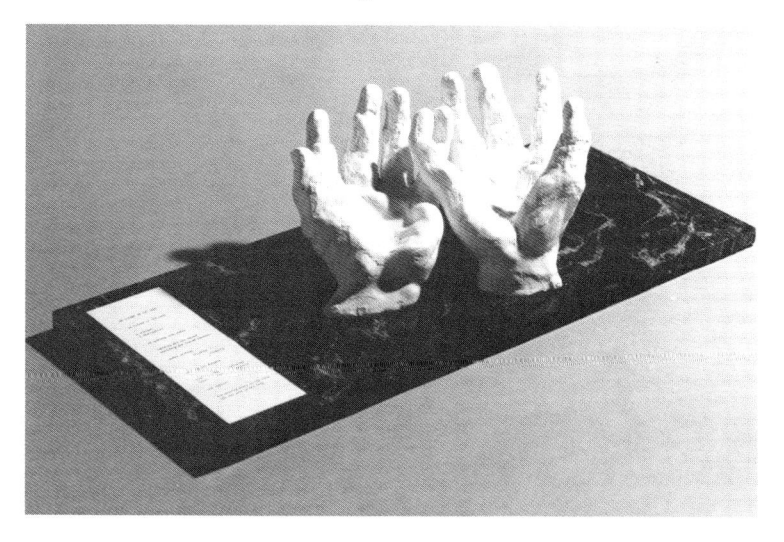

45

CHICAGO: ALTERNATIVE VISIONS

▶ **Redesign of Transit Facilities Recalling the Historic Significance of Chicago Transportation Buildings Old and New**
John E. Robbins

◀ **A River Refreshed**
David Rodemann

ALTERNATIVE VISIONS: CHICAGO

◀
Roof Garden Proposal to Aid in the Maintenance of the Ozone Layer
Liana A. Santoro

▶
The Superelevated: A Future Based on the Structure and Memory of Chicago's Past
John Ronan

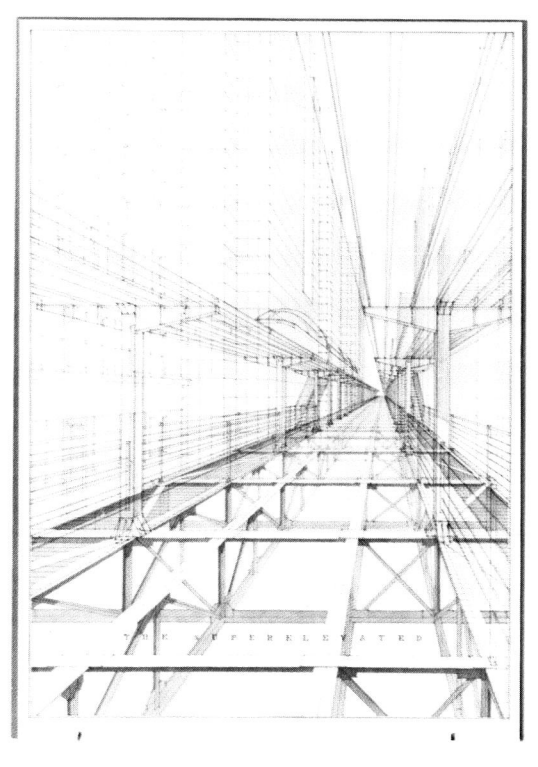

47

CHICAGO: ALTERNATIVE VISIONS

◄

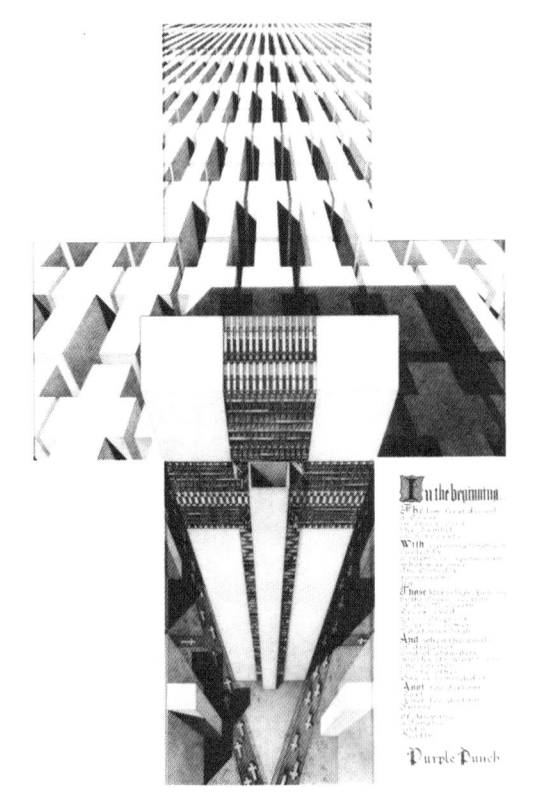

First Place

Untitled
Brian L. Shutz

▶

**Lake Shore Drive:
Edge vs. Barrier**
Waleed Shaalan

ALTERNATIVE VISIONS: CHICAGO

Sky Streets - Chicago
Neil J. Sheehan

Untitled
Randy Shear

CHICAGO: ALTERNATIVE VISIONS

▼
Untitled
Michael Louis Silver

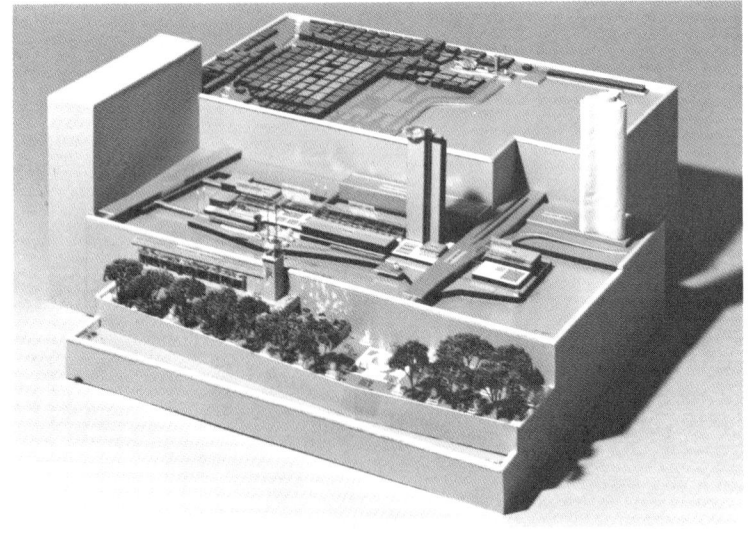

▲
**Lakefront Oasis -
Cradled in Blue
Water, Wrapped in
Skyscraper Steel -
A Return to Nature**
Stephen F. Smith

ALTERNATIVE VISIONS:

CHICAGO

◀
These Are the Best of Times and These Are the Worst of Times
Scott Sonoc

▶
Dearborn Street Bridge Tower: To Replace Existing Bridge Towers
Rene J. Stratton

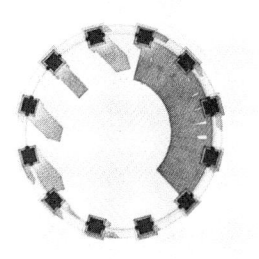

51

CHICAGO: ALTERNATIVE VISIONS

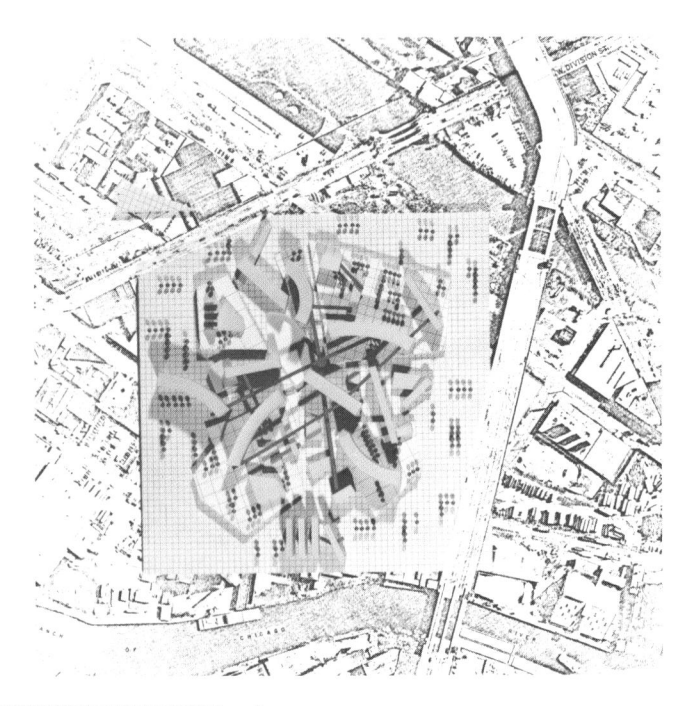

▼
World Expo 2000
Michael Stutz

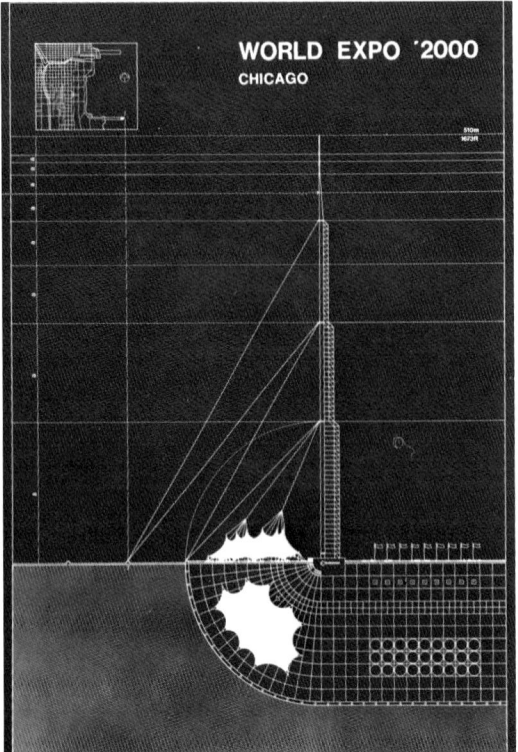

▲
Project for a Self-Sufficient Community on Goose Island
Daniel L. Tessarolo, Jr.

ALTERNATIVE VISIONS: CHICAGO

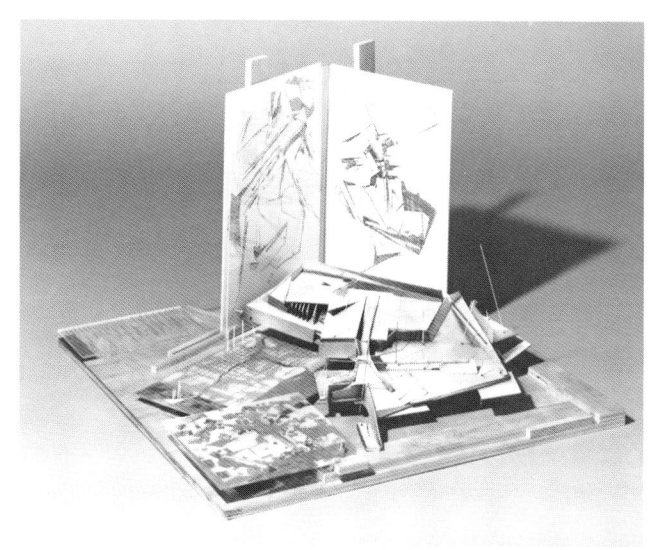

▼
Monument to the Homeless
Paul W. Todd

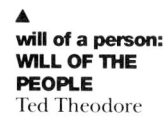

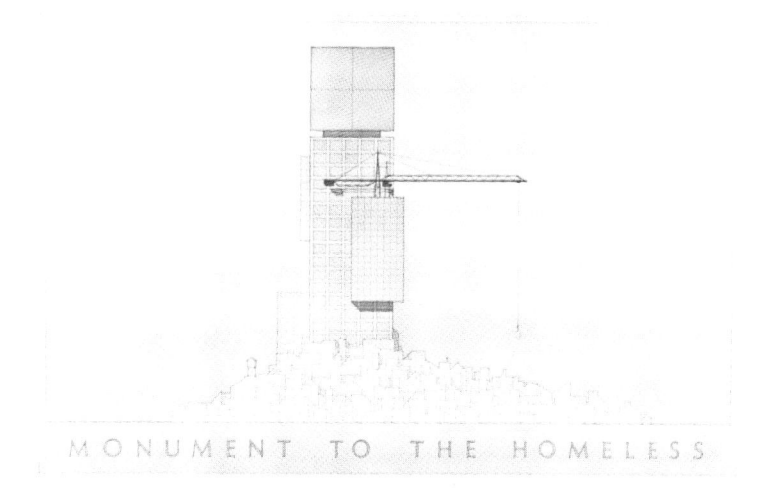

▲
will of a person: WILL OF THE PEOPLE
Ted Theodore

MONUMENT TO THE HOMELESS

53

CHICAGO: ALTERNATIVE VISIONS

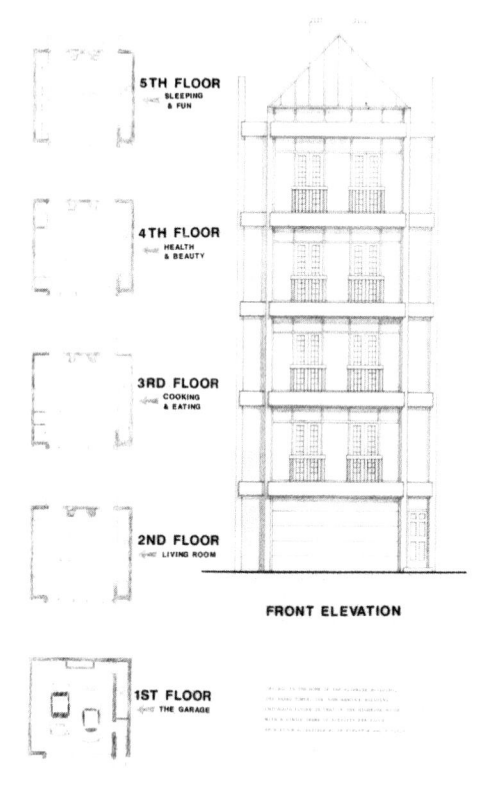

Untitled
Mark Van Spann

Venice of the North
Michael Venechuk

VENICE OF THE NORTH
DURING THE 1980'S THE CITY CHEERFULLY ADAPTED TO THE RISING WATERS OF LAKE MICHIGAN.

ALTERNATIVE VISIONS:

CHICAGO

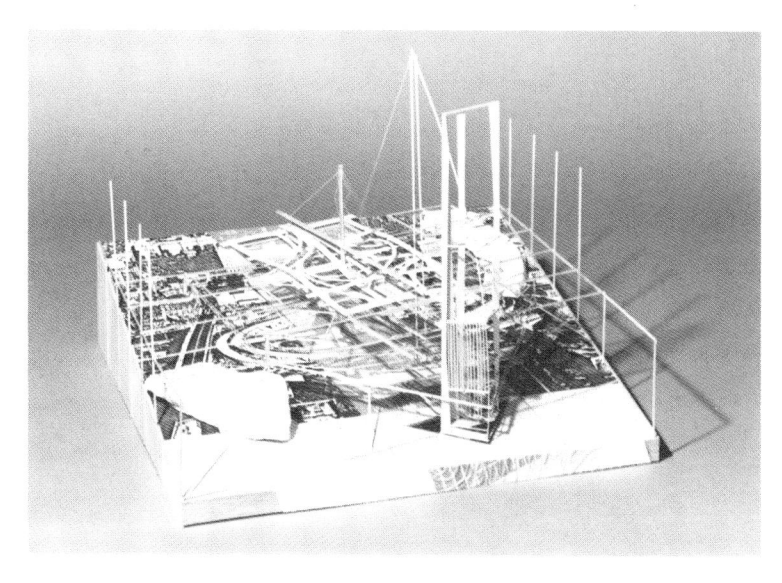

▲
**Theatre for Reading,
City of Chicago**
Amy Yurko

DBA

DISTINGUISHED BUILDING AWARD

DBA

The Chicago Chapter AIA Distinguished Building Awards program was initiated in 1955 and has become a model for similar programs in other AIA chapters across the country. The program recognizes significant achievement in planning, design and execution of building projects. Projects eligible for the 1989 program must have been completed between January 1986 and May 1989. They must be designed by registered architects with offices in the Chicago metropolitan area. The submissions themselves can be located anywhere in the world. The Awards jury is selected by the Design Committee. At the jury's discretion, a building may be selected to receive the special distinction of "Honor Award." From a separate pool of applicants, the same jury selects the Distinguished Restoration Award to honor excellence in the planning, design and execution of projects which have been restored to their original state.

JURY DBA

Clockwise from top left:
Deborah Berke, AIA
Berke & McWhorter Architects
New York, New York

Paul E. Dietrich, FAIA
Cambridge Seven Associates, Inc.
Cambridge, Massachusetts

Eric Owen Moss, AIA
Eric Owen Moss Architect
Culver City, California

**Jury Comments -
Distiguished Building Awards**

June 16, 1989

The Annual is a record of the activities of Chicago architects for the current year. It records all the works that Chicago architects submit to the Building and Interior Awards for the year. By looking at the entries, one can get a very good idea of what was happening that year in the Chicago design community.
The jury selects projects each year according to a standard arrived at in the course of the jury process, standards which are very dependent on the mix and chemistry of the jury for that year. Recently it has been noted that on national and local levels, it is difficult for a project over three stories to win an award.
Rather it is the summer cottages and small shops, or – as in the case of the 1989 Chicago Interior Architecture Awards, the apartment building laundry room – that are singled out for special recognition.
A partial explanation for this phenomenon lies in the reasons clients choose architects. Small project clients are unusual in that their projects often could have been done without a design architect. These clients need to have an extraordinary taste for good design in opting for an architect's services, and a high level of personal commitment to becoming a part of the ongoing design and decision-making process. For them, the reward is the individualized design and attention to detail that result from the close collaboration of architect and client.
Large project clients often choose an architect who will carry out their program, provide expertise in technical areas, and create a well-designed building that will not startle or call attention to itself. Clients often tell their architect, "I don't want an award-winning building." Companies that do want to make a design statement often choose a "brand name designer" with a recognizable design signature.
Jury members are chosen because their body of work stands apart from the pack on account of a long, distinguished career, high-visibility projects, and/or recent innovative work.
The aim of jury members is, more often than not, to choose winning entries that will demonstrate a highly

JURY COMMENTS DBA

individualized approach to design, an approach which has been executed based on the highest academic standards of the profession. Although jurors attempt to be egalitarian, inevitably their choices are shaped by their experience with various kinds of projects. As a result, this year's jury, as in other years, was chosen with an eye to diversity by the Design Committee. The 1989 Distinguished Building Award Jurors were Deborah Berke, of Berke and McWhorter Architects, New York, NY; Paul Dietrich, of Cambridge Seven Associates, Inc., Cambridge, Mass.; and Eric Owen Moss, of Eric Owen Moss, Architect, Los Angeles, California.

The first task for jury is to establish a procedure for reviewing the submissions and decide, within the definition of the award, how to select the winning entries. The general instructions are that they are to select the "best projects" and that they may, if they wish, make a distinction between honor awards and certificates of merit. But, as the jury gets acquainted, their own approach to the task takes form.

This year's jury felt that as architects jurying the work of their peers, they had to choose projects that were more than just competent or sensitive. For them, winning projects had to explore new solutions and establish new standards for excellence.

One theme that emerged from the 1989 jury was the issue of the "competent project." Paul Dietrich felt that it was important and right to award designs that are "straightforward, but appropriately well done in a direct, professional way. A project doesn't have to be 'cutting edge' to be distinguished." Deborah Berke's view was that "These are awards the profession gives to itself. Just to say that it is appropriately well-done is depressing. Every project ought to be well done. The profession needs to put a higher demand on itself than 'professionally well-done.'"

The projects at issue for this debate were the House Renovation by Dan Wheeler and the Ravinia Gift Shop by Lubotsky Metter Worthington and Law.

The House Renovation is a rebuilt boarding house, redesigned as a single-family house divided by a single courtyard. Paul Dietrich felt that the house was extremely well-done in all aspects of design. "The architect has taken a house designed for another use and converted it with sensitivity." Deborah Berke applauded the architect for "taking that enormous slice out of the center and opposing the two sections, like two parts of a dialogue. As a diagram, it reveals what an urban house might be today as opposed to when it was built."

Eric Moss noted that it was one of the few projects that supplied good drawings, including a section to be studied by the jury. But in general, he felt that it raised no important questions, broke no new ground.

The Ravinia Gift Shop designed by Jim Law, of the now disbanded firm of Lubotsky Metter Worthington + Law, is a small addition to an existing theatre building. Paul Dietrich and Deborah Berke argued in favor of the project. Paul called it a "nicely detailed adjunct which establishes a presence. It is nicely composed against the wall. It will sit there for a long time." Deborah felt that the shop was very successful as a composition. "It is opposed to the shed. The steel beam and the two trays create an opposition to the wall and the smokestack. It's a decent job in a serene location."

In opposition, Eric Moss felt strongly that the design did not go far enough. "It could have been more adversarial. It's too sedate. Decency doesn't get you an award. It doesn't push anything." He felt that "how it touches the building" was an important issue that had not been addressed.

DBA JURY COMMENTS

The Kinkead Pavilion of the Krannert Art Museum by Booth Hansen provoked a heated debate. The jury was strongly divided on the merits of the project, but finally presented an award because it had provoked the best conversation.

Two of the jurors had strong reservations about the project. Paul Dietrich made this assessment: "When I first saw the building up on the hill, I was enchanted. It troubles me that when we got inside, it fell apart. The galleries seem tight and unappealing. The narrow spaces and low ceiling contradict the interior. However, the fact that it served the need in creating a new image within the campus plan is significant."

Deborah Berke's reaction was, "I can't stand it. It represents what went disastrously wrong with investigations of post-modernism– the Charles Jenks formula of "take them out of the dusty file, blow them off, put them together." What separates it from the other projects of this type is that it is the only one that isn't trying to be like a polite house-guest–it's not using Postmodern forms in an ameliorative way. Yet I still don't like it."

Eric Moss was the strong advocate for this project. "This is the only project we've got that has an exploratory dimension–you don't need to like it. Discordant notes play if you are used to a different kind of harmony."

"Galleries don't HAVE to be enormous. It works. It's a straight piece. It's commendable as a try, and it explores the questions of what obligations the architect has, how to deliver those obligations, what is pastiche, what is the value of investigatory work."

Opinions aligned differently in the case of the Glendale Heights Post Office by Ross Barney Jankowski. One of the program requirements was that the design should help customers identify the building, in order to distinguish the facility from its neighbors.

Deborah Berke was its strongest champion. "It's hard to do a good post office on a limited budget. It takes the industrial park type and plays with it in a successful way. It is a billboard in its context–and the design has to do with announcing itself. Paul Dietrich agreed, and called it "A low-budget building done with fun and spirit. It is an appropriate solution that deserves recognition."

Eric Moss, on the other hand, felt that it was no more than a billboard done in "...conventional, known language. Color is substituted for thinking. The colors are distracting, taking away from what the object is. The geometry is most ordinary, and the Sesame Street level of coloration doesn't necessarily make it fun."

The Honor Award went to the only project on which all jurors were in agreement: The Hole in the Wall Gang Camp by Hammond Beeby Babka. The jurors liked the idea that different members of the design team were each given their own building to design, to give the project variety and make individual buildings distinctive. The program for the project was a key element in their choice.

Deborah Berke had mixed feelings about the project, but "given the user group, it is done very well. It is successful particularly because of its appropriateness to the people it serves. I find its greatest strength is in the site plan."

Eric Moss felt that it was a special kind of building done in a very sensitive and thoughtful way. "Something in the project has to do with the broadest ambitions of what architecture is about. This is a community, and it is friendly."

Paul Dietrich liked the idea of creating "this joyful setting." "There is a clear sense of appropriateness. It avoids the faults of Disneyland because of its purpose."

As in previous years, the jury found it very hard to approach the preservation/restoration

61

JURY COMMENTS DBA

entries. Some of the questions they raised were: Are we awarding technical competence? If there is an element of design and revision by the architect, does it still belong in the restoration category? Are we really awarding the original architect? What if we don't like his design?

The Union Station in Washington, D. C., received a Commendation in this category. The jury agreed that it gave new life and restored grandeur to a magnificent old building, and allowed it to function in today's commercial atmosphere. "It breathed new life into a corpse." Eric Moss summed it up: "It gives the spirit of city in a spatial sense back to the city to use–a public piece of the city. What architects are about is designing the city."

Jane Lucas
Executive Director
Chicago Chapter AIA

COMMERCIAL

DBA SUBMISSIONS

◄ **American Yazaki**
Canton Township, Michigan
Solomon Cordwell Buenz & Associates Inc.
Photo: Balthazar Korab

▲ **800 Fairway Drive**
Deerfield Beach, Florida
Solomon Cordwell Buenz & Associates Inc.
Photo: Keith Douglas

► **Corporate Place**
Nonconnah Corporate Center, Memphis, Tennessee
Nagle, Hartray & Associates, Ltd.
Photo: Marco Lorenzetti, Hedrich-Blessing

◄ **The Galleria at Erieview**
Cleveland, Ohio
Anthony Belluschi Architects, P.A.
Photo: Gregory Murphey

▼ **Commerce Plaza Entrance Pavilion**
Oak Brook, Illinois
Jack Train Associates Inc.
Photo: Hedrich-Blessing

63

DBA

SUBMISSIONS

COMMERCIAL

▶
The NBC Tower at Cityfront Center
Chicago, Illinois
Skidmore, Owings & Merrill
Photo: Hedrich-Blessing

▼
General Accident Insurance
Lisle, Illinois
Vickrey/Ovresat/Awsumb Associates, Inc.
Photo: Marco Lorenzetti, Hedrich-Blessing

◀
McDonald's Office Building
Oak Brook, Illinois
Lohan Associates
Photo: Nick Merrick, Hedrich-Blessing

▼
Market Tower
Indianapolis, Indiana
Lohan Associates
Photo: Nick Merrick, Hedrich-Blessing

▲
Northwestern Atrium Center
Chicago, Illinois
Murphy/Jahn
Photo: Timothy Hursley

64

DBA

SUBMISSIONS

COMMERCIAL

▶
Post Office Plaza Office Building
Somerville,
New Jersey
Anthony Belluschi
Architects, P.A.;
Gilligan &
Bubnowski
Architects, P.A.
Photo: Allan Weitz

◀
Park Avenue Tower
New York, New York
Murphy/Jahn
Photo: Nathaniel Lieberman

▼
One Liberty Place
Philadelphia,
Pennsylvania
Murphy/Jahn
Photo: John McGrail

▲
Oakbrook Urban Venture Theater/ Retail Building
Oak Brook, Illinois
Solomon Cordwell
Buenz & Associates
Inc.
Photo: Don DuBroff,
Sadin Photo Group

▶
Oakbrook Terrace Tower
Oak Brook, Illinois
Murphy/Jahn
Photo: George
Lambros

65

DBA SUBMISSIONS

COMMERCIAL

▶
Solo Cup Company Offices
Highland Park, Illinois
Serena-Sturm Architects, Ltd.
Photo: Steinkamp/Ballogg

▼
Ravinia Gift Shop
Highland Park, Illinois
Lubotsky Metter Worthington & Law, Ltd.
Photo: James Law

▲
6 West Hubbard Street
Chicago, Illinois
Griskelis & Smith Architects, Ltd.
Photo: David Clifton

◀
303 West Madison
Chicago, Illinois
Skidmore, Owings & Merrill
Photo: Steinkamp/Ballogg

◀
Westbrook Corporate Center
Westchester, Illinois
Schipporeit, Inc.
Photo: Barry Rustin

66

RESIDENTIAL

DBA SUBMISSIONS

Coleman Residence
Bannockburn, Illinois
Youngman & Company, Inc.
Photo: George Cambros

Davis House
Union Pier, Michigan
Peter Landon Architects
Photo: Wayne Cable

◄ **Belgravia Terrace Townhomes**
Chicago, Illinois
Gelick Foran Associates, Ltd.
Photo: Howard N. Kaplan

▲ **Edgewater Court**
Chicago, Illinois
Pappageorge Haymes, Ltd.
Photo: PHL

◄ **Farmhouse**
Lake Forest, Illinois
Booth/Hansen & Associates, Ltd.
Photo: Timothy Hursley, The Arkansas Office

67

DBA

RESIDENTIAL

◀
Larrabee Commons
Chicago, Illinois
Pappageorge
Haymes, Ltd.
Photo: PHL

◀
Lakeside "Boxcar" House
Lakeside, Michigan
Schroeder Murchie
Laya Associates, Ltd.
Photo: Gregory Murphey

▼
580 West Hawthorne Place
Chicago, Illinois
Schroeder Murchie
Laya Associates, Ltd
Photo: Leslie Schwartz

▲
Krug Residence
Barrington Hills, Illinois
Jaeger, Nickola & Associates Ltd., Architects
Photo: Jaeger, Nickola & Associates Ltd., Architects

68

RESIDENTIAL

DBA SUBMISSIONS

▼
Private Residence
Northfield, Illinois
Tigerman McCurry
Photo: Bruce Van Inwegen

◄
Prairie Court Apartments
Oak Park, Illinois
Nagle, Hartray & Associates, Ltd.
Photo: Marco Lorenzetti, Hedrich-Blessing

▼
Private Residence
Highland Park, Illinois
Stuart Cohen & Anders Nereim Architects
Photo: Nick Merrick, Hedrich-Blessing

◄
Marine Terrace
Chicago, Illinois
Pappageorge Haymes, Ltd.
Photo: PHL

DBA SUBMISSIONS

RESIDENTIAL

◀
Residence
Chicago, Illinois
Daniel Wheeler
Architects, Inc.
Photo: William
Kildow

▼
Residence
Highland Park,
Illinois
Nagle, Hartray &
Associates, Ltd.
Photo: Howard N.
Kaplan

▲
**Schiller Street
Townhouses**
Chicago, Illinois
Nagle, Hartray &
Associates, Ltd.
Photo: Howard N.
Kaplan

◀
River Cottages
Chicago, Illinois
Harry Weese &
Associates
Photo: Hedrich-
Blessing

RESIDENTIAL

DBA SUBMISSIONS

◄
Wolfson Residence
Northbrook, Illinois
Frye Gillan
Molinaro Architects, Ltd.
Photo: George Lambros

◄
Wits' End
Southwestern Michigan
Tigerman McCurry
Photo: Gregory Murphey

▼
Stremmel House
Sanibel Island, Florida
Riverside Architects
Photo: Howard N. Kaplan

▲
Walner Residence
Glencoe, Illinois
Arquitectonica Chicago, Inc.
Photo: Tim Street Porter

▲
2020 St. John's Residence
Highland Park, Illinois
David C. Hovey
Photo: Bill Hedrich, Hedrich-Blessing

71

DBA

SUBMISSIONS

RENOVATION

◄
Highland Park Farm
Highland Park,
Illinois
Nagle, Hartray &
Associates, Ltd.
Photo: Howard N.
Kaplan

▶
The Aldine Building
Chicago, Illinois
Lisec & Biederman,
Ltd.
Photo: Ron Gordon

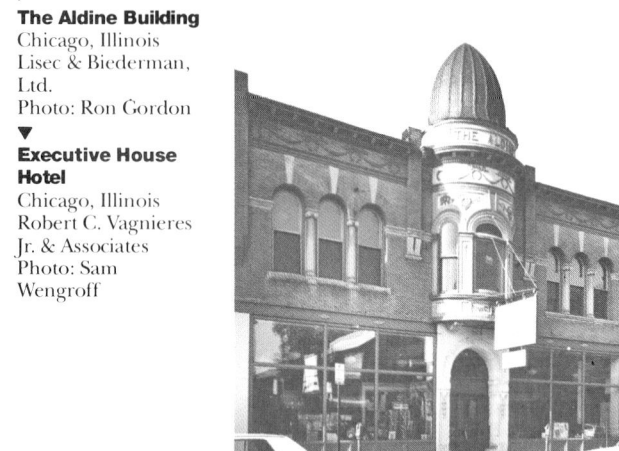

▼
Executive House Hotel
Chicago, Illinois
Robert C. Vagnieres
Jr. & Associates
Photo: Sam
Wengroff

◄
Cobbler Square
Chicago, Illinois
Schroeder Murchie
Laya Associates, Ltd.
Photo: David Clifton

▼
Federal Reserve Bank Expansion and Renovation
Chicago, Illinois
Holabird & Root
Photo: Nick Merrick,
Hedrich-Blessing

72

RENOVATION

DBA SUBMISSIONS

▲
Washington Square
Chicago, Illinois
Pappageorge
Haymes, Ltd.
Photo: Don DuBroff,
Sadin Photo Group
▶
North Pier Terminal
Chicago, Illinois
Booth/Hansen &
Associates, Ltd.;
The Austin Company,
Associate Architect
Photo: Wayne Cable,
Cable Studios;
Christopher Hinds

▲
Koren Building
Luther College
Decorah, Iowa
Weese Hickey Weese
Architects Ltd.
Photo: Jon Miller,
Hedrich-Blessing
◀
**Lake Forest College
Old North Gym**
Lake Forest, Illinois
O'Donnell,
Wicklund, Pigozzi
and Peterson
Architects, Inc.
Photo: Howard N.
Kaplan

◀
**Stewart Memorial
Library**
Coe College
Cedar Rapids, Iowa
Weese Hickey Weese
Architects Ltd.
Photo: Howard N.
Kaplan

73

DBA SUBMISSIONS

INSTITUTIONAL

◀ **Camp Algonquin**
Algonquin, Illinois
Tigerman McCurry
Photo: Bruce Van Inwegen

◀ **Capital High School**
Sante Fe,
New Mexico
Perkins & Will
Photo: Gregory Murphey

▼ **Clarke College Library/Fine Arts/ Chapel Complex**
Dubuque, Iowa
VOA Associates, Inc.
Photo: Bill Hedrich, Hedrich-Blessing

▲ **Arthur Andersen & Company Center for Professional Development**
St. Charles, Illinois
Skidmore, Owings & Merrill
Photo: Hedrich-Blessing

INSTITUTIONAL

DBA SUBMISSIONS

▼
Glendale Heights Post Office
Glendale Heights, Illinois
Ross Barney & Jankowski, Inc.
Photo: Barry Rustin

◄
Northwestern University Sports Pavilion and Aquatics Center
Evanston, Illinois
Holabird & Root
Photo: Timothy Hursley, The Arkansas Office

▼
Friendship Park Conservatory
Des Plaines, Illinois
Environ, Inc.
Photo: Wayne Cable, Cable Studios

▲
Northbrook Congregation Ezra-Habonim
Northbrook, Illinois
Jaeger, Nickola & Associates Ltd., Architects
Photo: Jaeger, Nickola & Associates Ltd., Architects

►
Kinkead Pavilion, Krannert Art Museum
University of Illinois
Champaign, Illinois
Booth/Hansen & Associates, Ltd.
Photo: Timothy Hursley, The Arkansas Office

75

DBA SUBMISSIONS

INSTITUTIONAL

▲
Trinity Lutheran Church
Lisle, Illinois
Jaeger, Nickola & Associates Ltd., Architects
Photo: Jaeger, Nickola & Associates Ltd., Architects

◄
Daniel F. and Ada L. Rice Building
The Art Institute of Chicago
Chicago, Illinois
Hammond Beeby and Babka
Photo: Jon Miller, Hedrich-Blessing

▲
Student Residence and Commons
University of Illinois at Chicago
Chicago, Illinois
Solomon Cordwell Buenz & Associates, Inc.
Photo:Steinkamp/Ballogg

◄
Parkside Lodge of Mundelein, East Wing Addition
Mundelein, Illinois
Rozovics & Associates; Richard Jay Solomon & Associates
Photo: Bob Shimer, Hedrich-Blessing

INDUSTRIAL

◀
Illinois Bell Telephone Equipment Building
Lisle-Naperville, Illinois
Holabird & Root
Photo: David Clifton

▶
Illinois Bell Telephone Equipment Building
Lincolnshire, Illinois
Holabird & Root
Photo: David Clifton

DBA SUBMISSIONS

MISCELLANEOUS

▼
Hole in the Wall Gang Camp
Ashford, Connecticut
Hammond Beeby and Babka
Photo: Timothy Hursley, The Arkansas Office

◀
Northbrook Commuter Station
Northbrook, Illinois
Richard Jay Solomon & Associates
Photo: Bob Shimer, Hedrich-Blessing

▲
Electromagnetic Interference Laboratory
Underwriters Laboratories
Northbrook, Illinois
Jack Train Associates Inc.
Photo: Barry Rustin

◀
Martin/Savage Studio
Oak Park, Illinois
Peter Landon Architects Ltd.
Photo: Wayne Cable, Cable Studios

MISCELLANEOUS

DBA SUBMISSIONS

▶
Ruskin Street Bathing Pavilion
Seaside, Florida
Stuart Cohen & Anders Nereim Architects
Photo: Robert Davis

▼
Rowes Wharf
Boston, Massachusetts
Skidmore, Owings & Merrill
Photo: Nick Wheeler

▼
St. Isidore Parish Facilities Building
Bloomingdale, Illinois
Harding Associates
Photo: Bruce Van Inwegen

▶
Regional Network Operations Center
Chicago, Illinois
Teng & Associates, Inc.
Photo: William Kildow

79

DBA SUBMISSIONS

MISCELLANEOUS

◄
630 Vernon Avenue
Glencoe, Illinois
David C. Hovey
Photo: Bill Hedrich,
Hedrich-Blessing

◄
Waste Management Environmental Monitoring Laboratories, Inc.
Geneva, Illinois
Perkins & Will
Photo: George Lambros

▲
The Willows
Chicago, Illinois
Pappageorge Haymes, Ltd.
Photo: PHL

▶
1770 First Street
Highland Park, Illinois
David C. Hovey
Photo: Scott McDonald, Hedrich-Blessing

DISTINGUISHED RESTORATION

DRA SUBMISSIONS

Emmel Building
Chicago, Illinois
Michael J. Pado AIA Architect, Ltd.
Photo: Michael J. Pado

Illinois State Capital Restoration
Springfield, Illinois
Graham, Anderson, Probst & White, Inc.
Photo: Graham, Anderson, Probst & White, Inc.

Union Station
Washington, DC
Harry Weese & Associates
Photo: Carol M. Highsmith

St. Clement's Church
Chicago, Illinois
Holabird & Root
Photo: Don DuBroff, Sadin Photo Group

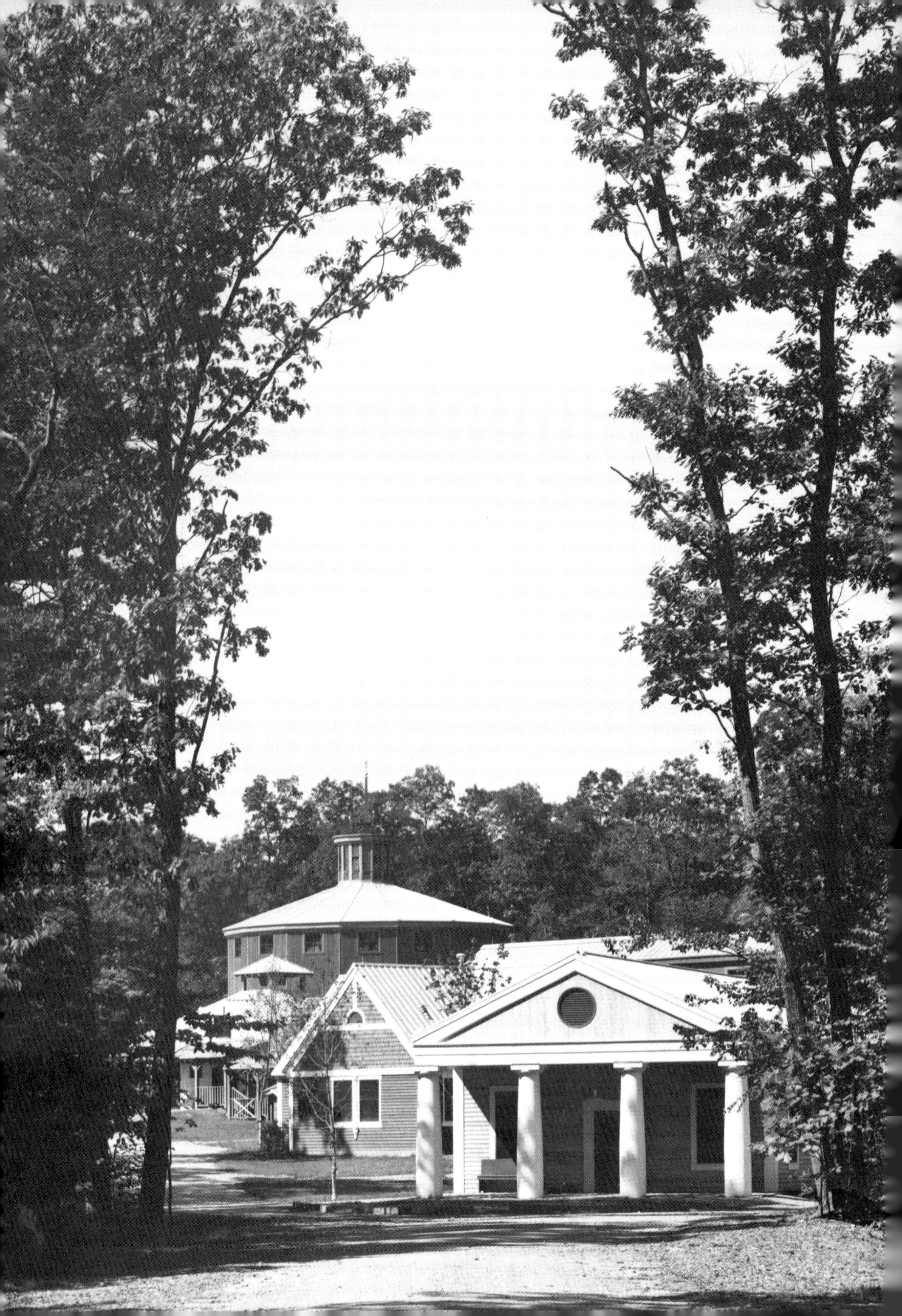

DBA HONOR AWARD

Hole in the Wall Gang Camp
Ashford, Connecticut

Hammond Beeby and Babka

Project Team: Gary M. Ainge, *Principal in Charge and Project Architect*; Thomas H. Beeby, *Director of Design*; Bernard F. Babka, *Director of Technical, Production, and Office Practice*; Phillip J. Liederbach, Kirk R. Stevens, David K. Jurina
Client: Hole in the Wall Gang Camp Fund - Newman's Own, Inc.
Contractor: Konover Construction Corporation
Interior Design Consultants: Langdon & Woodhouse, Architects
Associate Architect: Russo + Sonder
Structural Engineer: Getty, White & Mason
Mechanical/Electrical Engineer: Sarracco, Inc.
Photographer: Timothy Hursley

Paul Newman founded this camp for children with life-threatening illnesses. His goal was to provide a full outdoor experience for those whose physical condition would normally rule out that possibility. The arrangement of the camp is based on a cinematographic unfolding of space and buildings that recalls images of rural and frontier settlements. Figural buildings seen along controlled vistas serve as landmarks to orient campers in their daily routines. The architectural setting refers to the full spectrum of American vernacular building traditions.

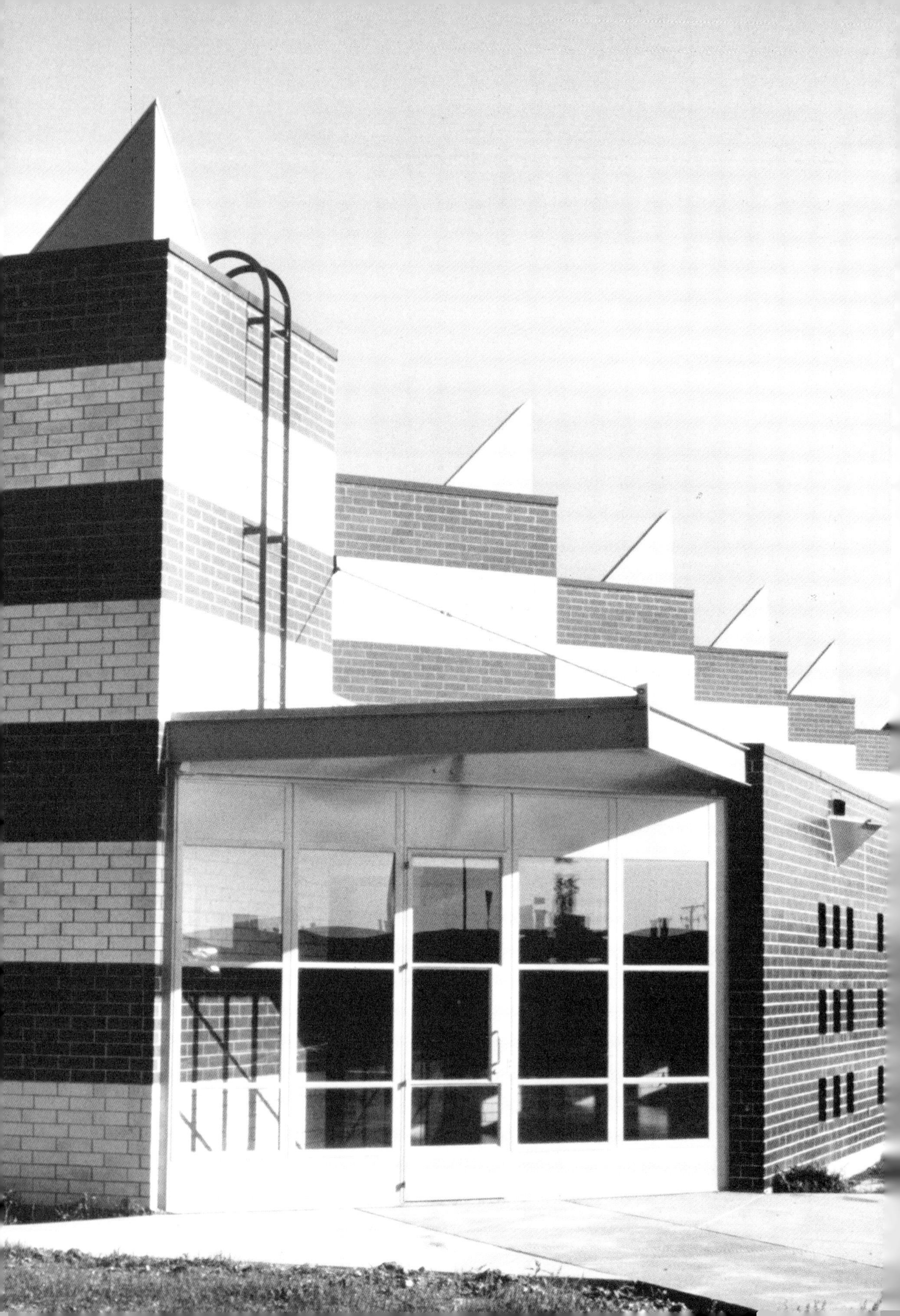

Glendale Heights Post Office
Glendale Heights, Illinois

Ross Barney + Jankowski, Inc.

This 24,000-square-foot suburban post office is the only retail operation in a warehouse-filled industrial park. The design seeks to distinguish the facility from its neighbors, while maintaining the red and buff brick palette of the park.

Since the first impression of the building is from the adjacent highway, the facade is scaled to be comprehended at forty-five miles per hour. Striped walls enclose the workroom and carrier parking. A blue-glazed brick wall defines the service and lockbox lobbies; it is punctuated with a field of small openings that admit light while screening an uninspiring view of parking lots. Skylights illuminate the entrances to lockbox bays.

Bright gold screens mark the workroom skylights on the facade. The triangular forms are repeated as roof scuppers.

Inside, the "Stars and Stripes" theme is carried out in the exposed striped brick walls and patterned linoleum flooring.

Project Team: Carol Ross Barney, AIA; James C. Jankowski, AIA
Client: United States Postal Service
Contractor: Delko Construction Company
Structural Engineer: Martin/Martin
Mechanical/Electrical Engineer: Beling Consultants
Photographer: Barry Rustin

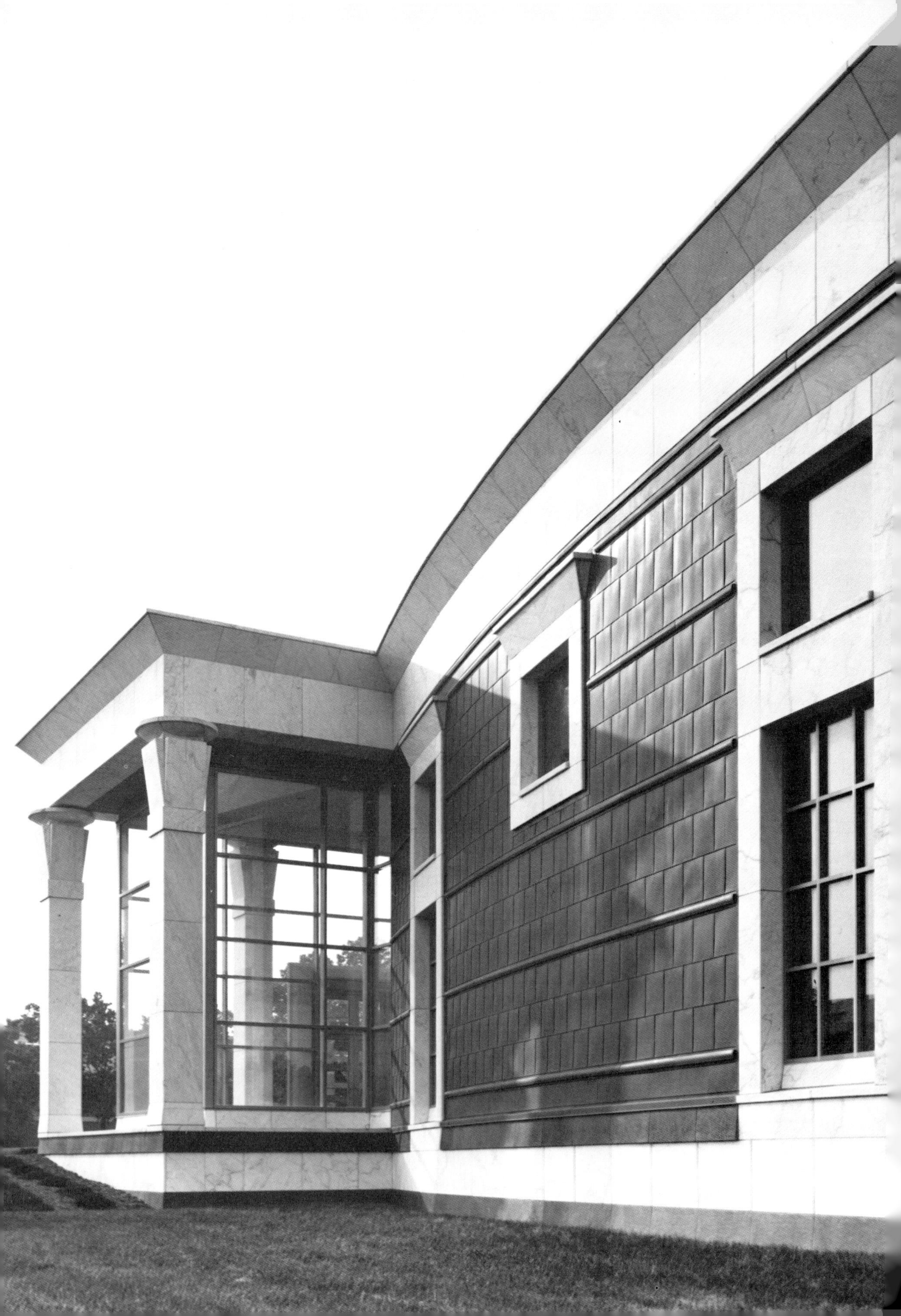

**Kinkead Pavilion, Krannert Art Museum
University of Illinois
Champaign, Illinois**

Booth/Hansen & Associates, Ltd.

Project Team: Laurence Booth, *Design Principal*; Paul Hansen, *Managing Principal*; Virginia Kinnucan
Client: University of Illinois
Contractor: English Brothers Company
Structural Engineer: Beer, Gorski & Graff
Mechanical/Electrical Engineer: Gamze Korobkin Caloger, Inc.
Photographer: Timothy Hursley, The Arkansas Office

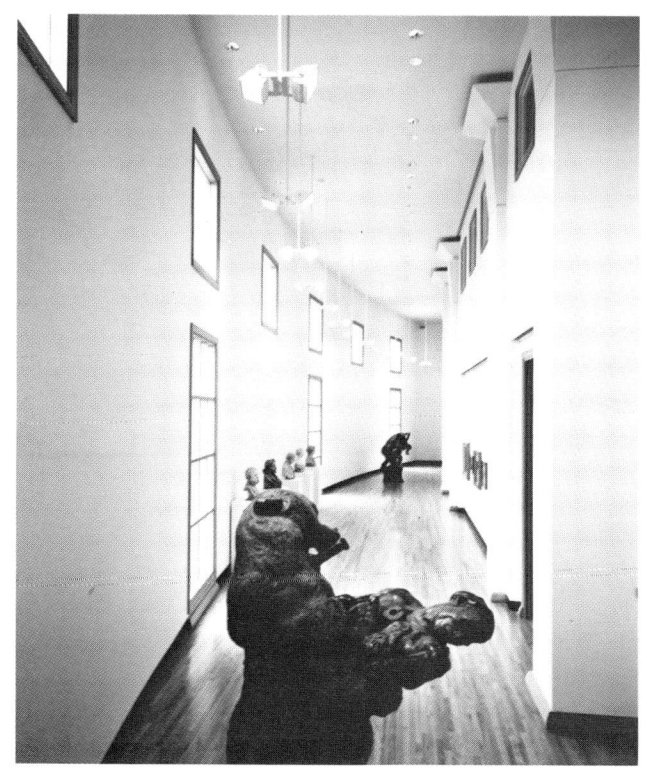

The Kinkead Pavilion provides an additional 20,000 square feet of exhibition, study, administrative, and storage space for the existing Krannert Art Museum.
The pavilion's siting and design integrate the museum with student pathways and visually connect the surrounding buildings. A repositioned and more prominent entrance makes the building more accessible to the main campus quadrangle.
Upper level windows allow natural light into the galleries without sacrificing control over exhibition lighting. Rich primary materials–copper, marble, and oak–harmonize with the Georgian campus and ensure durability.

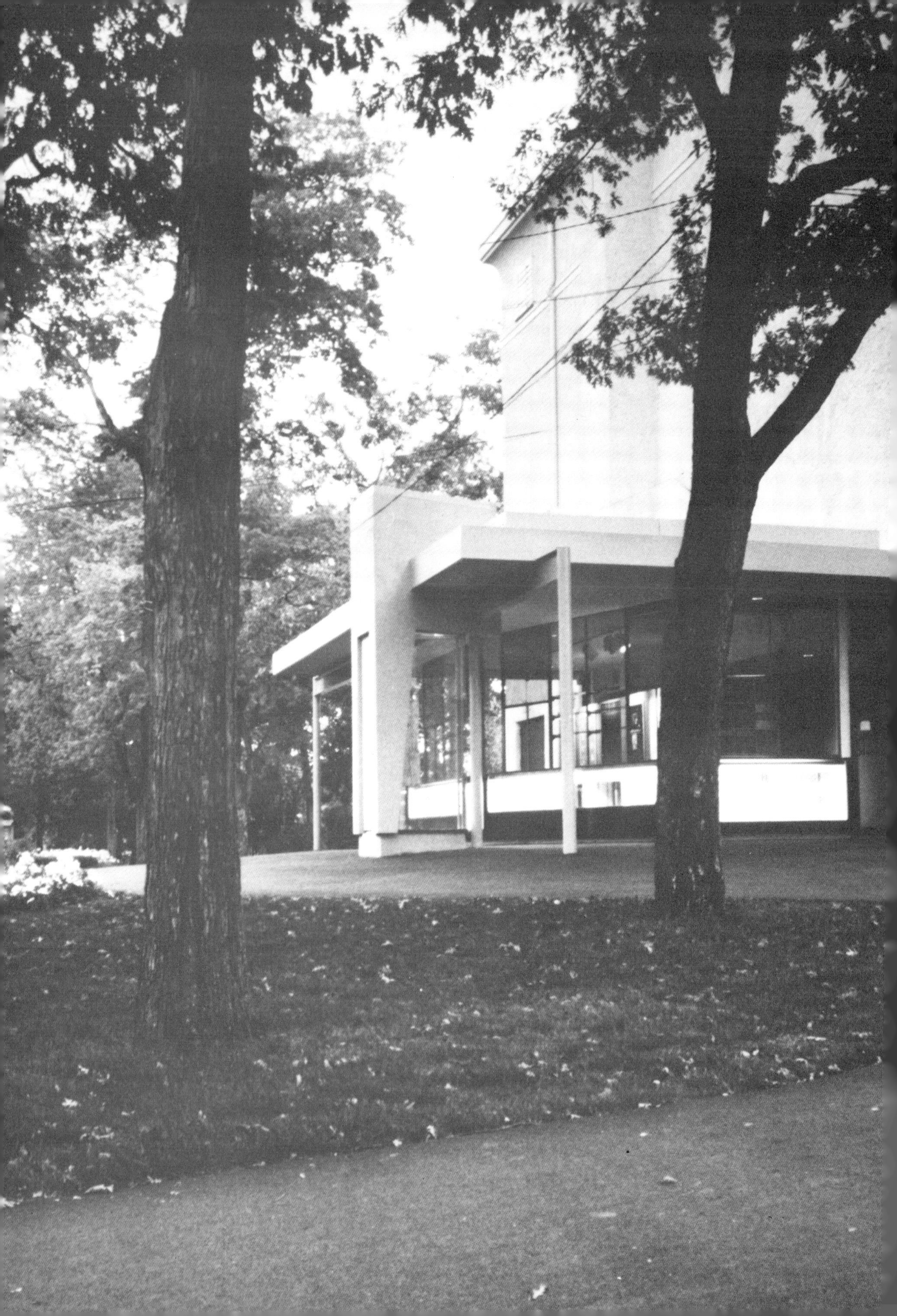

Ravinia Gift Shop
Highland Park, Illinois

Lubotsky Metter Worthington + Law, Ltd.

Project Team: James Law, Andrew Metter, Robert Lubotsky, Wayne Worthington, Skip Smith
Client: Ravinia Festival Association
Contractor: Stratton Inc.
Structural Engineer: Seymour Lepp Associates
Mechanical Engineer: Brian Berg Associates
Electrical Engineer: Dickerson Engineering
Photographer: James Law

For a gift shop on the site of an outdoor summer music festival, the design had to strike a balance between the visual impact necessary to encourage souvenir sales and a low-key background presence to avoid distraction during performances.

The scheme takes its inspiration from Ravinia's heavily wooded natural setting. By day, the shop is a minimal and abstract composition set against a large neutral wall. The large expanses of glass, exposed structure, and horizontal roof with deep overhangs respond to the airiness of the surrounding oak trees and their leafy canopies. At night, the shop becomes a volume of light, highlighting displayed objects. The roof canopy, a shield from sun and rain during the day, at night becomes a reflective ceiling surface which emits a warm glow of light visible to both pavilion and lawn audiences.

DBA CERTIFICATE OF MERIT

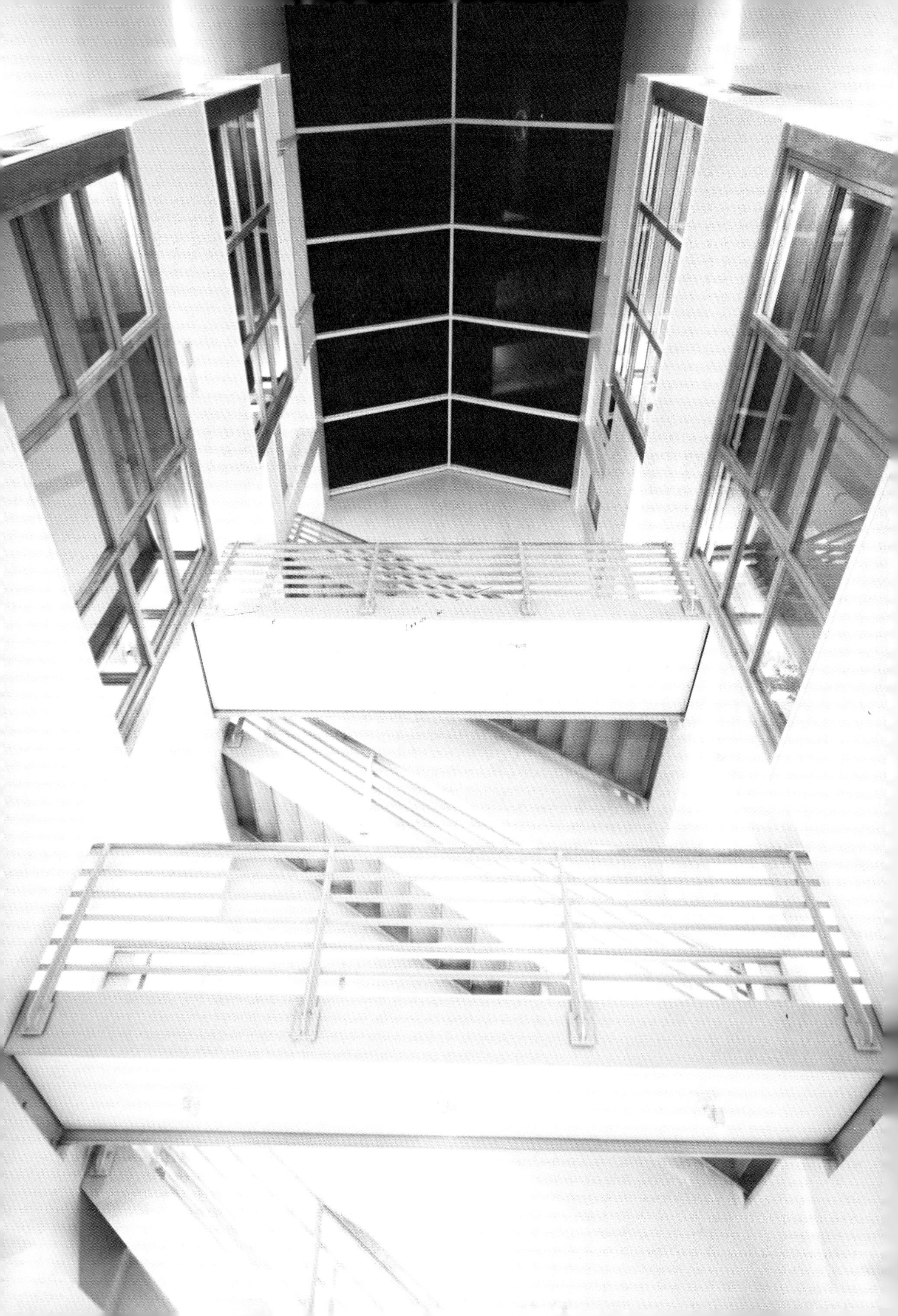

Residence
Chicago, Illinois

Daniel Wheeler Architects, Inc.

Project Team: Daniel Wheeler, Brad Erdy, Lawrence Kearns, Liza Bachrach, Francis Mullen
Client: The Kissner Development Company/Private Owner
Contractor: The Kissner Company
Structural Engineer: Scott Leopold
Mechanical Engineer: Paul Keissling
Landscape Architect: Maria Whiteman

A long, lightless boarding house has been rebuilt into a single residence, conceived as two houses sharing an internal courtyard.
The house presents a series of articulated rooms, detailed quietly, to form a backdrop for the play of the sun and the moon. Naturally finished maple and granite provide warmth and a sense of scale to prominent, accessible surfaces, while structural steel elements provide cool contrast.
Wooden bays, projecting into the courtyard, capture the sunshine by day, and in the evening become lanterns for the dining room below.

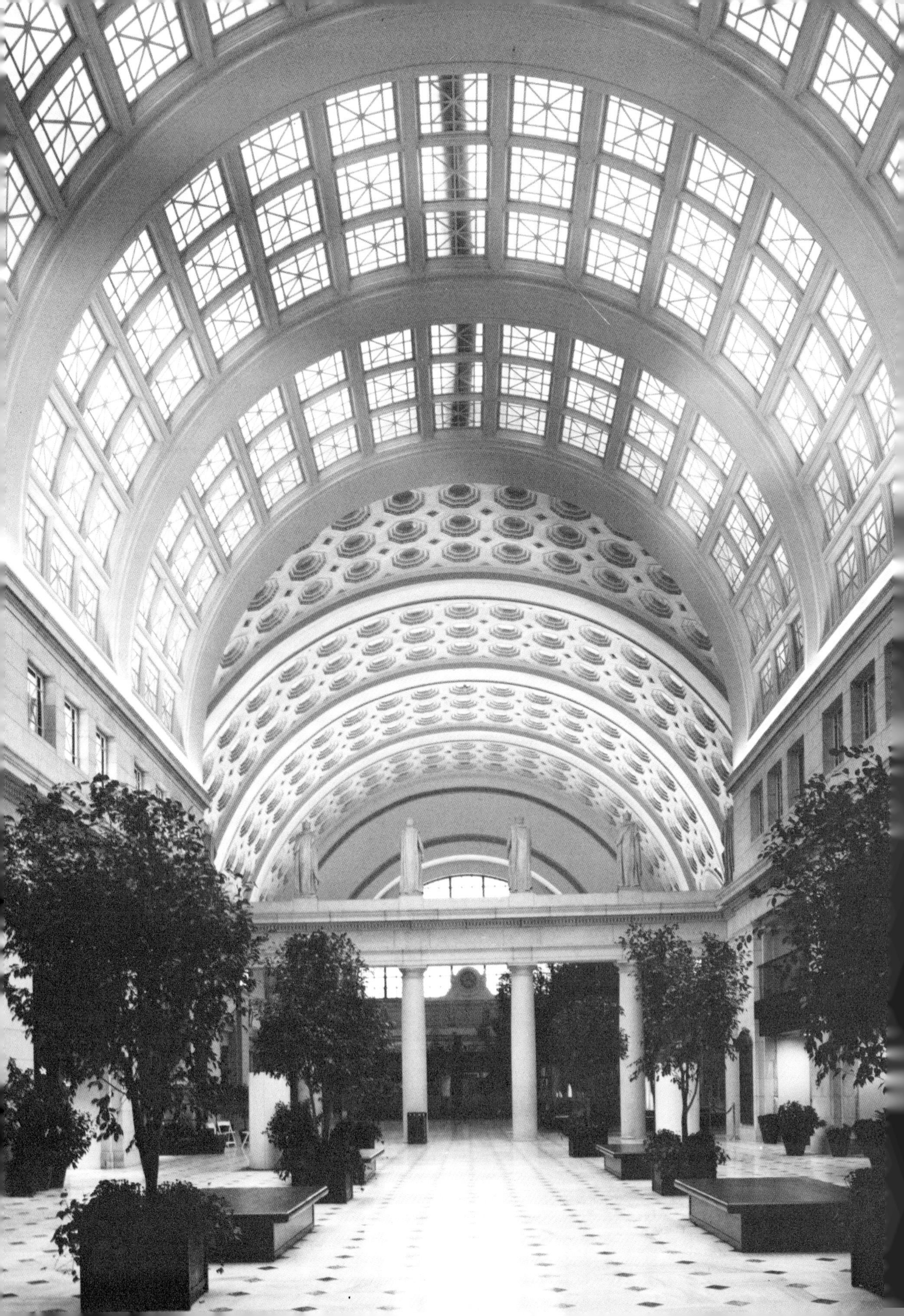

Union Station
Washington, D.C.

Harry Weese & Associates

Union Station by Daniel Burnham (1904) is in the classical tradition of the Ecole des Beaux Arts and is distinguished by its coffered vault. By the early seventies, because of deferred maintenance and misguided renovation, coinciding with a decline in passenger use, the structure was declared unsafe.
In 1981, Congress initiated a redevelopment program, returning the public spaces to their original grandeur, with special attention to floor materials, ornamentation, decorative stenciling, as well as lighting. The original Burnham drawings guided what has been called the largest historically accurate restoration in the United States.
A new parking garage and vehicular ramps link to the station concourse. In the lower levels, the extensive reclaimed area accommodates commercial and retail spaces.

Project Team: Harry Weese & Associates
Client: Union Station Redevelopment Corporation
Consulting Architect: Fry & Welch Associates
Contractor: Dick Corporation
Mechanical Engineer: John L. Christie & Associates
Structural Engineer: Tippetts-Abbett-McCarthy
Electrical Engineer: H.C. Yu and Associates
Consulting Engineer: Wiss, Janney, Elstner Associates
Photographer: Carol M. Highsmith

IAA

INTERIOR

ARCHITECTURE

AWARD

IAA

The Chicago Chapter AIA Interior Architecture Awards program was initiated in 1980 to recognize excellence in interiors work in Chicago, and to celebrate interior architecture as a unique discipline. For the purpose of these awards, interior architecture is defined as the design of space within a building envelope, including the design of lighting, finishes, and furnishings. Interior architecture projects completed and constructed during the period of January 1, 1986 to March 1, 1989 were eligible.

JURY IAA

Clockwise from top left:
Joseph D'Urso
D'Urso Design, Inc., East Hampton, New York

Linda Nelson, AIA
Department of Interior Architecture, School of the Art Institute of Chicago
Keene Nelson Keene

Charles Pfister, AIA
The Pfister Partnership, San Francisco, California

COMMERCIAL
OFFICE

IAA SUBMISSIONS

◄
American National Can
ISD Incorporated
Photo: Nick Merrick,
Hedrich-Blessing

▲
Bayer Bess Vanderwarker
Weese Hickey Weese Architects Ltd.
Photo: Peter Vanderwarker

◄
August Bishop & Meier
Garapolo & Associates,
Schmitt/Cibulka Associates
Photo: Steinkamp/Ballogg Chicago

▲
Alcar Incorporated
Serena-Sturm Architects, Ltd.
Photo: Steinkamp/Ballogg Chicago

97

IAA

SUBMISSIONS

COMMERCIAL
OFFICE

◀
Jim Beam Brands Co.
Swanke Hayden Connell Ltd.
Photo: Jon Miller, Hedrich-Blessing

◀
Bond Brewing/ G. Heileman
F.I. Torchia Associate
Photo: James Yochur

▲
Branch Bank
Bauhs and Dring, Ltd.
Photo: Bill Crofton

▶
Carson Pirie Scott and Company
The Amistad Group, Inc.
Photo: Jeff Atkins, Mercury Studios

COMMERCIAL
OFFICE

IAA SUBMISSIONS

▼ **Eisaman, Johns & Laws**
Larson Associates
Photo: Gregory Murphey

▲ **E.I. DuPont de Nemours and Company**
Eva Maddox Associates, Inc.
Photo: Jon Miller, Hedrich-Blessing

◄ **Commerce Plaza Redevelopment Entrance Pavilion**
Jack Train Associates Inc.
Photo: Bill Hedrich, Hedrich-Blessing

◄ **Equitable Financial Group**
Interprise
Photo: David Clifton

99

IAA SUBMISSIONS

COMMERCIAL
OFFICE

▶
Federal Reserve Bank of Chicago Renovation and Addition
Holabird & Root
Photo: Nick Merrick, Hedrich-Blessing

▲
Firestone Corporate Headquarters
PHH Environments
Photo: Abby Sadin, Sadin Photo Group

▶
Foote Cone & Belding
The Landahl Group Inc.
Photo: Jon Miller, Hedrich-Blessing

▲
Fishman & Merrick, P.C.
Perkins & Will
Photo: Bruce Van Inwegen

100

COMMERCIAL OFFICE

IAA SUBMISSIONS

▲
Offices of Jardine, Emett & Chandler Illinois, Inc.
Johnson . Rogatz . Wilson
Photo: David Clifton

▼
Frankel & Company
Perkins & Will
Photo: Marco Lorenzetti, Hedrich-Blessing

▼
JMB Realty Corporation Headquarters
Griswold, Heckel & Kelly Associates, Inc.
Photo: Jamie Padgett, Karant & Associates

▼
IBM Midwest Region--Real Estate and Construction Division Offices
Gelick Foran Associates, Ltd.
Photo: Orlando Cabanban

▲
The Hearn Company
F.I. Torchia Associates
Photo: James Yochum

SUBMISSIONS IAA

COMMERCIAL
OFFICE

◀
Latham & Watkins
Booth/Hansen &
Associates
Photo: Wayne Cable,
Cable Studios

◀
Paul Libman Music Studio
Richard Jay Solomon
& Associates
Photo: Hedrich-Blessing

▼
Lotus Development Corporation
Mekus Johnson, Inc
Photo: Jon Miller,
Hedrich-Blessing

▲
Jones Day Reavis & Pogue
ISD Incorporated
Photo: Nick Merrick,
Hedrich-Blessing

COMMERCIAL
OFFICE

IAA SUBMISSIONS

▼
McBride Baker & Coles
Swanke Hayden Connell, Ltd.
Photo: Jon Miller, Hedrich-Blessing

▲
McConnaughy Barocci Brown
Krueck & Olsen Architects
Photo: Hedrich-Blessing 
◄
The McCord Group
E. R. Associates, Ltd.
Photo: William Kildow

◄
Law Offices of Mayer, Brown & Platt
Powell/Kleinschmidt, Inc.
Photo: Jon Miller, Hedrich-Blessing

103

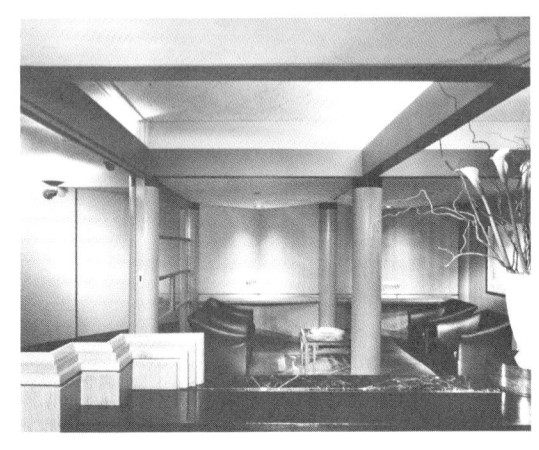

COMMERCIAL OFFICE

▼
Mekus Johnson, Inc., Design Offices
Mekus Johnson, Inc.
Photo: Jon Miller, Hedrich-Blessing

▲
Nagelberg & Resnick, P.C.
E.R. Associates, Ltd.
Photo: Jamie Padgett, Karant & Associates

▲
McKinley Financial Group & Republic Savings Bank
Interprise
Photo: David Clifton

▶
The Mitsui Trust and Banking Company, Ltd.
Hague-Richards Associates, Ltd.
Photo: Jon Miller, Hedrich-Blessing

COMMERCIAL OFFICE

IAA SUBMISSIONS

▶
Jeffrey Nemetz & Associates
Himmel/Bonner Architects
Photo: Wayne Cable

◀
Perkins & Will
Perkins & Will
Photo: Marco Lorenzetti, Hedrich-Blessing

▼
Pansophic Systems, Inc.
F.I. Torchia Associates, Inc.
Photo: James Yochum

▲
OMT Corporation
ISD Incorporated
Photo: Nick Merrick, Hedrich-Blessing

▶
Near North Title Company
Skidmore, Owings & Merrill
Photo: Nick Merrick, Hedrich-Blessing

IAA SUBMISSIONS

COMMERCIAL OFFICE

▶
Rivkin Radler Dunne & Bayh
Swanke Hayden Connell, Ltd.
Photo: Nick Merrick, Hedrich-Blessing

◀
Rudnick & Wolfe
Swanke Hayden Connell, Ltd.
Photo: Jon Miller, Hedrich-Blessing

▲
Rynne House Communications, Inc.
Criezis Architects
Photo: Judy A. Slagle

▶
Offices of Frederick Phillips & Associates
Frederick Phillips & Associates
Photo: Howard N. Kaplan

106

COMMERCIAL OFFICE

▼ **Sherman & Howard**
ISD Incorporated
Photo: Chas McGrath

▲ **The Sanwa Bank, Ltd.**
Hague-Richards Associates, Ltd.
Photo: Jon Miller, Hedrich-Blessing

▶ **Shearson Lehman Brothers**
Skidmore, Owings & Merrill
Photo: Hedrich-Blessing

▼ **Sidley & Austin**
ISD Incorporated
Photo: Nick Merrick, Hedrich-Blessing

▲ **Shearson Lehman Hutton, Inc.**
Hague-Richards Associates, Ltd.
Photo: Jon Miller, Hedrich-Blessing

107

IAA SUBMISSIONS

COMMERCIAL
OFFICE

▶
SSPS, Inc.
Mekus Johnson, Inc.
Photo: Jon Miller,
Hedrich-Blessing

▲
Stotler & Company
Perkins & Will
Photo: Marco
Lorenzetti, Hedrich-
Blessing
◀
**Stone Container
Corporation**
ISD Incorporated
Photo: Nick Merrick,
Hedrich-Blessing

▲
Source, Inc.
Pappageorge
Haymes Ltd.
Photo: Don DuBroff,
Sadin Photo Group

IAA SUBMISSIONS

C O M M E R C I A L
O F F I C E

▴
Westpac Banking Corporation
Techno, Ltd.
Photo: Paul Schlismann
▾
WGCI Radio
The Amistad Group, Inc.
Photo: Jeff Atkins, Mercury Studios

▴
Westminster Place
Hanno Weber & Associates
Photo: William Kildow
▴
The Winnetka Bank Main Office Remodeling
Bank Structures, Inc.
Photo: Samuel Fein

◂
Vedder, Price, Kaufman & Kammholz
VOA Associates, Inc.
Photo: Jeff Atkins

109

IAA

SUBMISSIONS

RETAIL & HOSPITALITY

▼
Backstreet Bar & Grill
Gelis & Associates, Inc.
Photo: Alice Q. Hargrave

▲
America's Kitchen
Aumiller Youngquist, P.C.
Photo: Steinkamp/Ballogg Chicago

◄
Bally of Switzerland
Perkins & Will
Photo: Abby Sadin, Sadin Photo Group

◄
Attitudes
Eckenhoff Saunders Architects
Photo: Bruce Van Inwegen

RETAIL &
HOSPITALITY

IAA SUBMISSIONS

Benedict's Restaurant
Loebl Schlossman and Hackl, Inc.
Photo: Steinkamp/Ballogg Chicago

◄ **Bridgewater Commons**
Anthony Belluschi Architects, Ltd.
Photo: Alan Schindler

▼ **Chiasso**
Florian-Wierzbowski Architecture, P.C.
Photo: Wayne Cable, Cable Studios

▲ **Cityscape**
Aumiller Youngquist, P.C.
Photo: Steinkamp/Ballogg Chicago

111

IAA SUBMISSIONS

RETAIL &
HOSPITALITY

▼
**First Chicago
Dearborn Station
Branch**
Griswold, Heckel &
Kelly Associates, Inc.
Photo: Jamie Padgett,
Karant & Associates

▲
Kinney Wallcoverings Showroom
Eastlake Studio, Inc.
Photo: Steve Hall,
Hedrich-Blessing
▶
**G.F. Furniture
Systems Showrooms**
Skidmore, Owings
& Merrill
Photo: Nick Merrick,
Hedrich-Blessing

▶
Glasses, Ltd.
Himmel/Bonner
Architects
Photo: Wayne Cable

112

RETAIL & HOSPITALITY

IAA SUBMISSIONS

◄ **Eddie Rockets**
Keane Nelson
Keane Architects
Photo: Keane

▼ **Oilily**
Florian-Wierzbowski
Architecture, P.C.
Photo: Wayne Cable

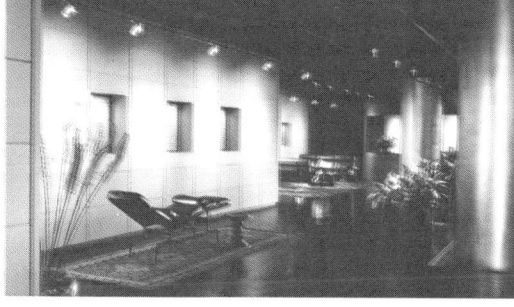

▲ **Stationery Station**
Daniel Wheeler
Architects
Photo: William Kildow
Photography

Herman Miller Showroom
Skidmore, Owings &
Merrill
Photo: Nick Merrick,
Hedrich-Blessing

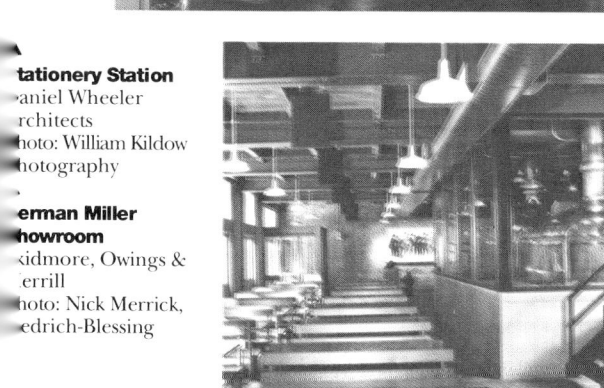

◄ **Sieben's River North Brewery**
Wallace Bowling
Architects
Damato/Kapusta
Associates, Architects
of Record
Photo: Kardas
Photography

113

RETAIL & HOSPITALITY

◀
Mary Walter
Urban Resource
Photo: Howard N. Kaplan

▲
Toshiro
James, Morris & Kutyla
Photo: Les Boschke

◀
Tereza
Pappageorge Haymes, Ltd.
Photo: PHL

▲
Turandot
The Office of Richard J. Gorman, AIA
Photo: George Lambros Photography

114

RENOVATION & ADAPTIVE REUSE

IAA SUBMISSIONS

▼
Camp Madron Lodge
Daniel Wheeler Architects
Photo: William Kildow Photography

◄
BMT Design
Pappageorge Haymes, Ltd.
Photo: Wayne Cable

▲
American Airlines Terminal Renovation
Anthony Belluschi Architects, Ltd.
(design phases only)
Photo: Don DuBroff, Sadin Photo Group

◄
Adaptive Office Reuse - Market Square
Hanno Weber & Associates
Photo: William Kildow

115

IAA SUBMISSIONS

RENOVATION &
ADAPTIVE REUSE

▼
**Lake Shore
Country Club**
Office of John
Vinci, Inc.,
with Marilyn Rubin,
Interior Decorator
Photo: Don DuBroff,
Sadin Photo Group

◄
**One East Wacker
Drive**
Lucien Lagrange &
Associates, Ltd.
Photo: George
Lambros

▼
**Executive Offices
of the Chicago
Mercantile
Exchange**
Powell/Kleinschmidt
Inc.
Photo: Jon Miller,
Hedrich-Blessing

◄
**O'Connor &
Associates**
PHH Environments
Photo: Wolfgang Hoyt

RENOVATION & ADAPTIVE REUSE

▶
Oriental Theater Remodeling
Quinn and Searl, Architects
Photo: George Lambros Photography

▼
122 South Michigan Avenue
Eckenhoff Saunders Architects
Photo: Bruce Van Inwegen

▼
State-Lake Theater
Skidmore, Owings & Merrill
Photo: Nick Merrick, Hedrich-Blessing

▶
Sedelmaier Productions, Inc.
Nagle Hartray & Associates, Ltd.
Photo: Nick Merrick, Hedrich-Blessing

IAA

SUBMISSIONS

RENOVATION &
ADAPTIVE REUSE

▶
Tang Industries
Arquitectonica
Chicago, Inc.
Photo: Steinkamp/
Ballogg

▼
Suite 301
Tainer Associates, Ltd.
Photo: Wayne Cable

▼
Roy O. West Library Renovation at De Pauw University
Weese Hickey Weese Architects, Ltd.
Photo: Wayne Cable, Cable Studios

▶
Woodwork Corporation of America
Powell/Kleinschmidt, Inc.
Photo: Jon Miller, Hedrich-Blessing

RESIDENTIAL

IAA SUBMISSIONS

▶
Chicago Residence
Michael Lustig & Associates, Inc.
Photo: Hedrich-Blessing

▶
Dunes Summer House Interiors
Frye Gillan Molinaro Architects, Ltd.
Photo: Gregory Murphey

▼
Bronstein Residence
Pappageorge Haymes, Ltd.
Photo: Wayne Cable

▲
The Finn Residence
Johnson . Rogatz . Wilson
Photo: David Clifton

◀
The Duncan Residence
Johnson . Rogatz . Wilson
Photo: Barbara Karant, Karant & Associates, Inc.

IAA SUBMISSIONS

RESIDENTIAL

▼
The New York Lobby
Banks/Eakin
Architects
Photo: Steinkamp/
Ballogg Chicago

▲
**580 West
Hawthorne Place**
Schroeder Murchie
Laya Associates, Ltd.
Photo: Leslie Schwartz
▶
**LaBarge Townhouse
Remodeling**
Quinn and Searl,
Architects
Photo: George
Lambros Photography

▶
**North Shore
Residence**
Stuart Cohen and
Anders Nereim
Architects
Photo: Nick Merrick,
Hedrich-Blessing

RESIDENTIAL

IAA SUBMISSIONS

▶
Residence
Powell/Kleinschmidt, Inc., and Rugo/ Raffensperger, Ltd.
Photo: Tony Soluri
▼
Przyborowski Residence
Eckenhoff Saunders Architects, Inc.
Photo: Don DuBroff, Sadin Photo Group

◀
Residence
Daniel Wheeler Architects
Photo: William Kildow

▲
Private Residence
Langdon & Woodhouse, Architects
Photo: Judith Bromley

IAA

SUBMISSIONS

RESIDENTIAL

▼
Sage Residence
Himmel/Bonner
Architects
Photo: David Clifton

▲
Stremmel House
Riverside Architects,
Ltd.
Photo: Howard N.
Kaplan
▶
Walner Residence
Arquitectonica
Photo: Timothy
Hursley

▲
Untitled #1
Krueck & Olsen
Architects
Photo: Hedrich-
Blessing
◀
**Residence of the
British Consul
General**
Harry Weese &
Associates
Photo: Jon Miller,
Hedrich-Blessing

INSTITUTIONAL

IAA Submissions

▼
"Chicago Architecture: 1872-1922"
Tigerman McCurry
Photo: Bruce Van Inwegen

**ole in the Wall
ang Camp Interiors**
angdon &
oodhouse, Architects,
interior design
onsultants to
ammond, Beeby &
abka, Inc., Architects
noto: Judith Bromley

▲
Nathan Cummings Outpatient Center
Hansen Lind Meyer, Inc.
Photo: Don DuBroff, Sadin Photo Group
◄
Circle Campus Student Commons Building
University of Illinois at Chicago
Eva Maddox Associates, Inc.
Photo: Nick Merrick, Hedrich-Blessing

123

IAA SUBMISSIONS INSTITUTIONAL

▶
Lutheran General Medical Group Offices - Buffalo Grove
Criezis Architects
Photo: Demetrios Criezis

▲
Schaumburg Township Public Library Addition & Renovation
O'Donnell Wicklund Pigozzi and Peterson Architects, Inc.
Photo: OWP&P Architects

◀
Rush-Presbyterian St. Luke's at the Atrium
Hansen Lind Meyer Inc.
Photo: Don DuBroff Sadin Photo Group

MISCELLANEOUS

IAA SUBMISSIONS

◀
Bell Communications Technical Education Center
O'Donnell Wicklund Pigozzi and Peterson Architects, Inc.
Photo: Abby Sadin, Sadin Photo Group

▲
E.I. Dupont de Nemours and Company
Eva Maddox Associates, Inc.
Photo: Jon Miller, Hedrich-Blessing

◀
Central Synagogue
Michael Lustig & Associates, Inc.
Photo: Steinkamp/ Ballogg

▲
AWS/Steil, Inc.
Eva Maddox Associates, Inc.
Photo: Nick Merrick, Hedrich-Blessing

The HON Company Showroom
ISD, Inc.
Photo: Nick Merrick, Hedrich-Blessing

Helikon Furniture Company, Inc.
Eva Maddox Associates, Inc.
Photo: Nick Merrick, Hedrich-Blessing

Oakbrook Terrace Tower Health Club
The Landahl Group, Inc.
Photo: Jon Miller, Hedrich-Blessing

MISCELLANEOUS

IAA Submissions

▼
Yacht
Atwood Architects
Photo: Robert Boler

◄
Regents Park Laundrette
Julie Thoma, Inc.
Photo: Judith Bromley
▼
United Airlines Red Carpet Club, Concourse C
Hague-Richards Associates, Ltd.
Photo: Jon Miller, Hedrich-Blessing

▲
United Airlines Red Carpet Club, Concourse B
Hague-Richards Associates, Ltd.
Photo: Nick Merrick, Hedrich-Blessing

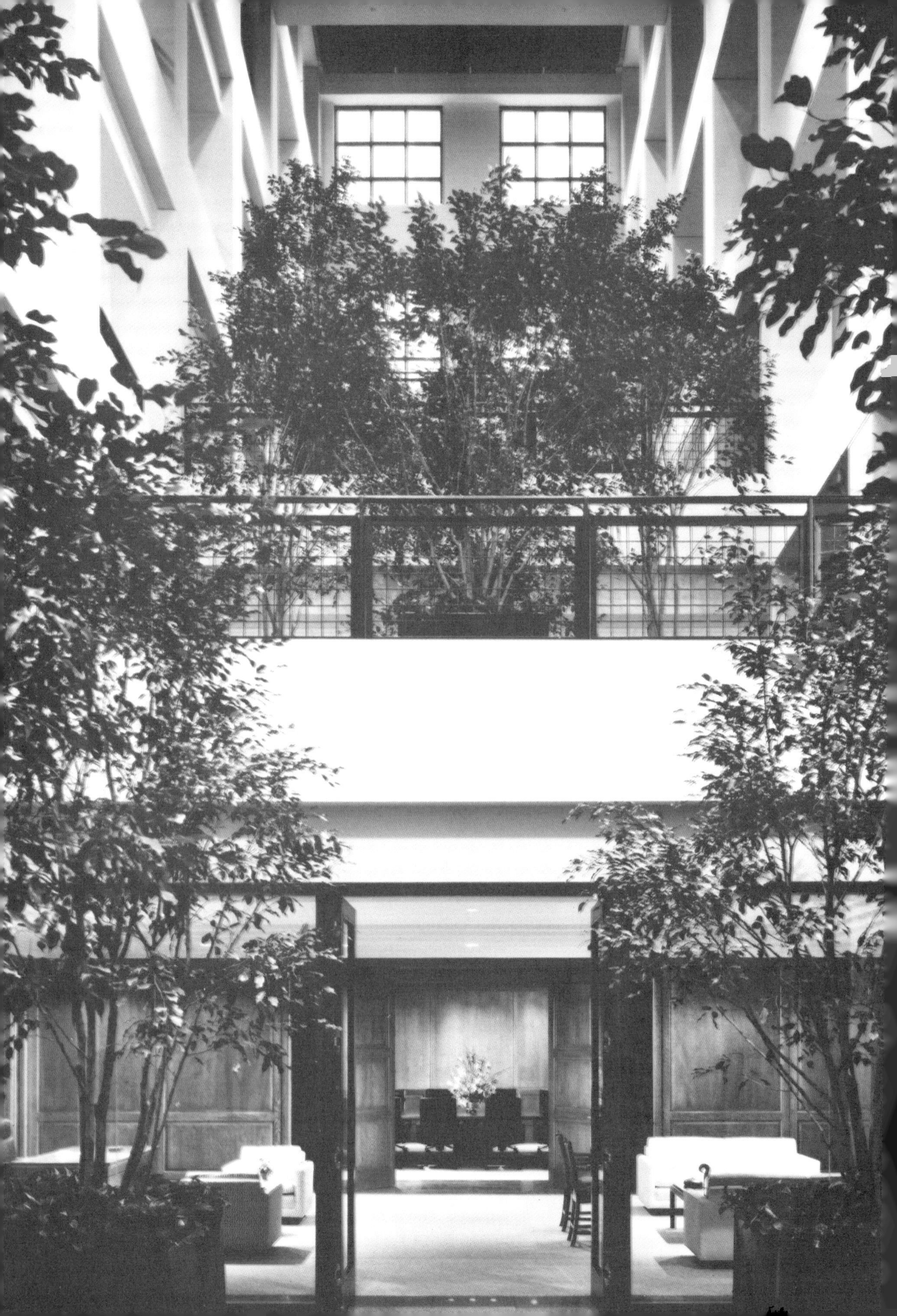

IAA HONOR AWARD

Federal Reserve Bank of Chicago Expansion and Renovation
Chicago, Illinois

Holabird & Root

Project Team: Eugene Cook, *Partner in Charge;* Gerald Horn, *Design Partner;* Jeff Case, *Project Manager;* Michael Pancost, *Project Architect;* Sharon Gonzalez, *Director of Interior Design;* Frank Scalia, *Interiors Project Coordinator*
Client: Federal Reserve Bank of Chicago
Contractor: Pepper Construction Company
Mechanical/Electrical Engineer: Environmental Systems Design, Inc.
Photographer: Nick Merrick, Hedrich-Blessing

This 1,000,000-square-foot bank occupies two existing buildings and an infill addition. The challenge was to restore and enhance the neoclassical decor of the 1920s lobby, create a new design vocabulary for the rest of the building, and humanize the vast 50,000-square-foot floors. In the restored 1920s Great Hall, new metal railings and custom carpet reflect an existing Roman cross motif. The Roman cross is reduced to a simple grid for the newer spaces. Two stepped atria open up the typical office floors with minimal sacrifice of space. Work stations are designed in modules of two, three and four units linked by a power spine. Burgundy, navy, and hunter green are used as dominant accent colors on alternating floors.

Jury Comments: "Very elegant... I would like to work there... stays consistent at all different levels, from public space to work space–that's an accomplishment... complicated project..."

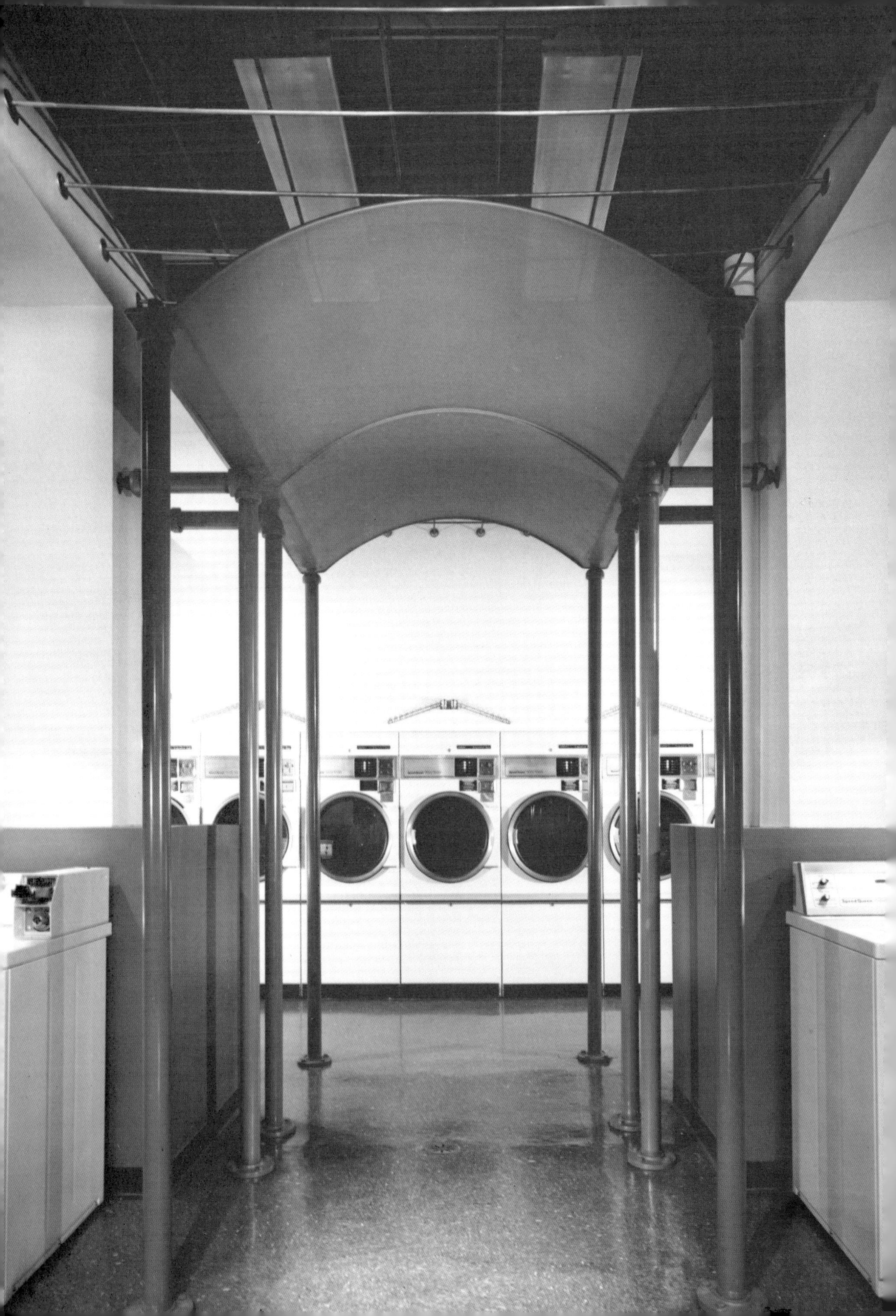

IAA HONOR AWARD

Regents Park Laundrette
Chicago, Illinois

Thoma, Incorporated

Project Team: Julie Thoma, Amy Lohmolder
Client: The Clinton Company
Contractor: Ben Cruz, Regents Park by The Clinton Company
Photographer: Jamie Padgett, Karant & Associates

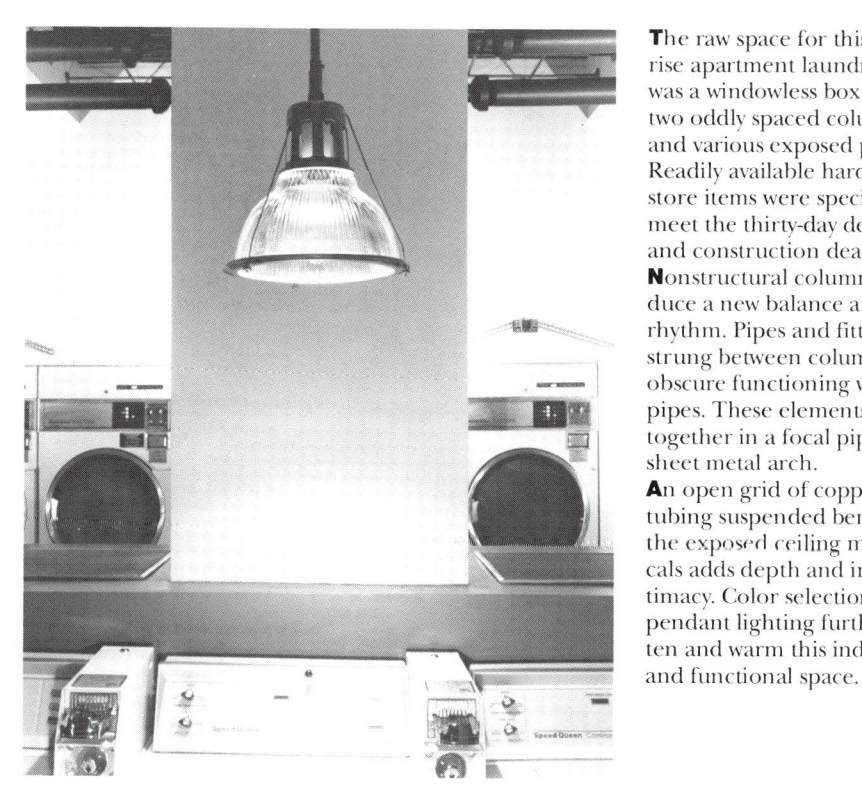

The raw space for this high-rise apartment laundrette was a windowless box with two oddly spaced columns and various exposed pipes. Readily available hardware store items were specified to meet the thirty-day design and construction deadline. **N**onstructural columns introduce a new balance and rhythm. Pipes and fittings strung between columns obscure functioning water pipes. These elements come together in a focal pipe and sheet metal arch.
An open grid of copper tubing suspended beneath the exposed ceiling mechanicals adds depth and intimacy. Color selections and pendant lighting further soften and warm this industrial and functional space.

Jury Comments:
"Fabulous, fresh... loving attention to a usually unattended-to space, on no money...a star is born"

131

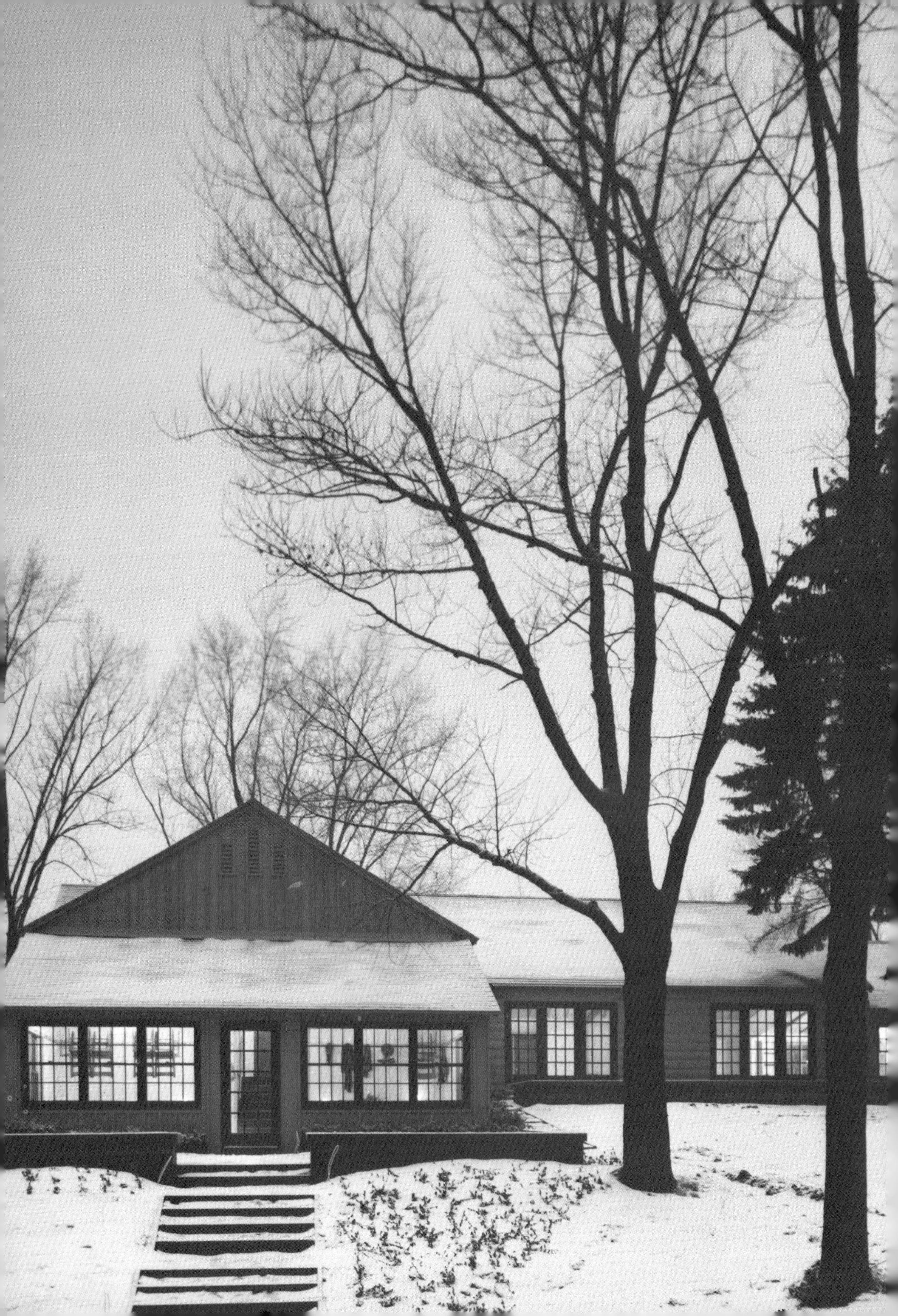

Nancy A. Adams Lodge
Camp Madron
Buchanan Township, Michigan

Daniel Wheeler Architects

Project Team: Daniel Wheeler, Brad Erdy, Lawrence Kearns, Liza Bachrach, Francis Mullen
Client: Horwitz Matthews
Contractor: Superior Builders
Structural Engineer: Howard Stearn
Mechanical Engineer: Mid-Continent Engineering
Photographer: William Kildow

The dilapidated lodge of an abandoned boy scout camp has been restructured to provide shelter, warmth and a place for comraderie in a new utopian community in southwestern Michigan.
Once an internalized sequence of murky rooms, the lodge has been opened to bring breezes and sunlight into spaces of simple utility. The rooms overlook a rolling landscape complete with fireflies in the evening.
A straightforward plan includes a warming room, great hall, dining room, and a community reading room for perusing tall tales by the fire.
Detailing, materials, and palette all grew from a reflective study of the rural landscape. It is intended to wear long and well.

Jury Comments: "Glad it exists... pure, restrained, very "shaker" space... very simple wood structure that has been edited beautifully..."

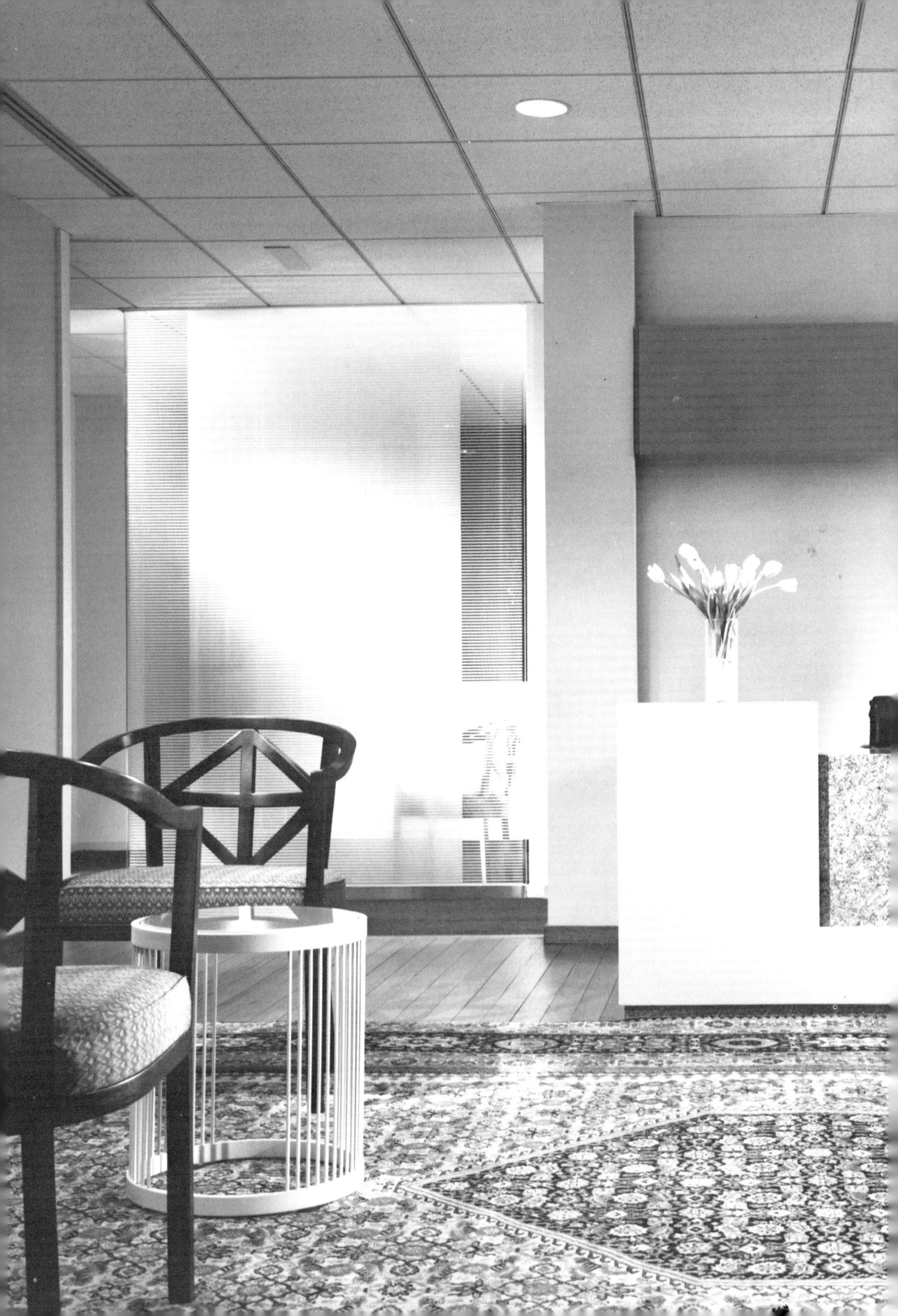

IAA

CERTIFICATE OF MERIT

**Frankel & Company
Chicago, Illinois**

Perkins & Will

Showcasing the creative energy and extensive portfolio of an advertising agency while maintaining a limited budget was the design problem for the 32,000-square-foot office.
The dramatic character of the elevator lobby, which features glass walls illuminated with neon, extends to the reception area, where the lobby's archway is reflected in the design of the main desk. An oriental rug on an Australian eucalyptus floor produces a warm and welcoming atmosphere for clients and guests.
Glass-fronted offices alternating with conventionally enclosed offices provide visual variety in the corridors. Centrally located presentation areas are easily accessible to staff and accommodate creative "brainstorming."
A multi-purpose room with state-of-the-art audio-visual capabilities for client presentations includes darkroom and computer graphics facilities and rear-screen projection.

Jury Comments:
"Masterful organization... lightness, simplicity... clean... really comes off as a space..."

Project Team: Neil P. Frankel, AIA, *Design Principal*; Catherine D'Hoostelaere, *Project Manager*; James Prendergast, Joanne Bauer, Yetta Starr, *Team*
Client: Frankel & Company
Contractor: Turner Construction Company, Special Projects Division
Mechanical/Electrical Engineer: Cosentini Associates
Audio-Visual Consultants: ISR Inc.
Photographer: Marco Lorenzetti, Hedrich-Blessing

135

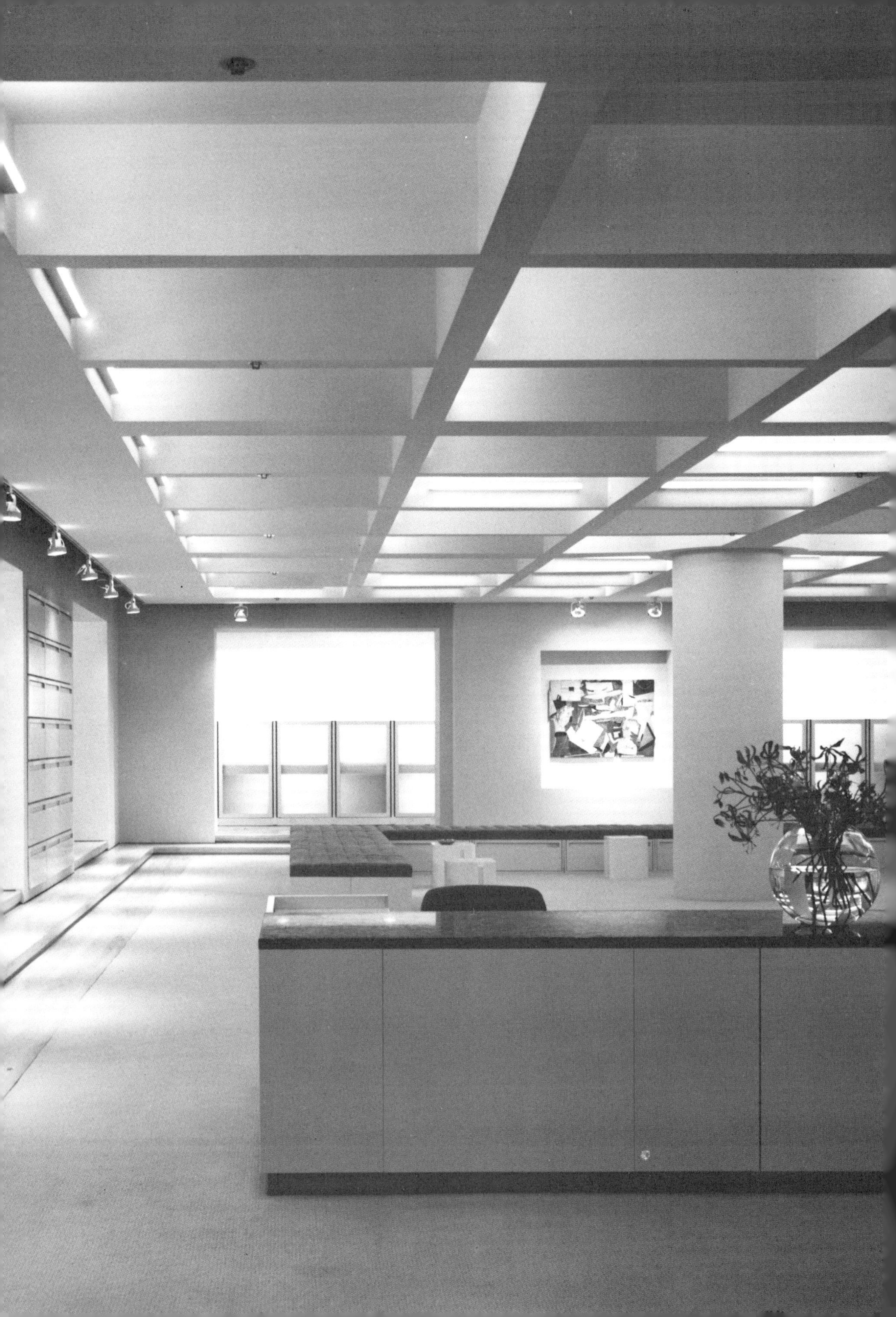

IAA

CERTIFICATE OF MERIT

GF Furniture Systems Showrooms
Chicago, Illinois

Skidmore, Owings & Merrill

Project Team: Bruce J. Graham, *Design Partner;* William M. Drake, *Project Partner;* Patrick McConnell with Michelle Mirrielees, *Design;* Hal Scheffers with Michael Bonhart, *Technical;* William N. Larson, *Project Management*
Client: GF Furniture Systems
Contractor: Merchandise Mart Properties
Photographer: Nick Merrick, Hedrich-Blessing

Jury Comments: "Such a classic, so serene... you hardly notice the materials because the materials are the structure... very special place to inspire young designers that with a can of white paint and good organization you can do a good job... enormously successful as a showroom..."

A deliberately simple series of showroom spaces were designed to highlight GF's classic line of office furniture. **A** spacious entrance loggia opens to the grand showroom, a versatile central area for product display. The smaller showrooms, alternately square and circular, symmetrically flank the central room providing defined areas for product settings, wall displays of fabric samples, and client mock-ups. **F**inished in beige and white and infused with natural light, the showroom provides a neutral, glowing backdrop for the varied colors and textures of GF's product line. Elements that interact with light–lattice doors, a suspended grid ceiling, plaster walls, etched glass–quietly animate the space and complement the natural materials used– white oak, buff wool and white silk.

137

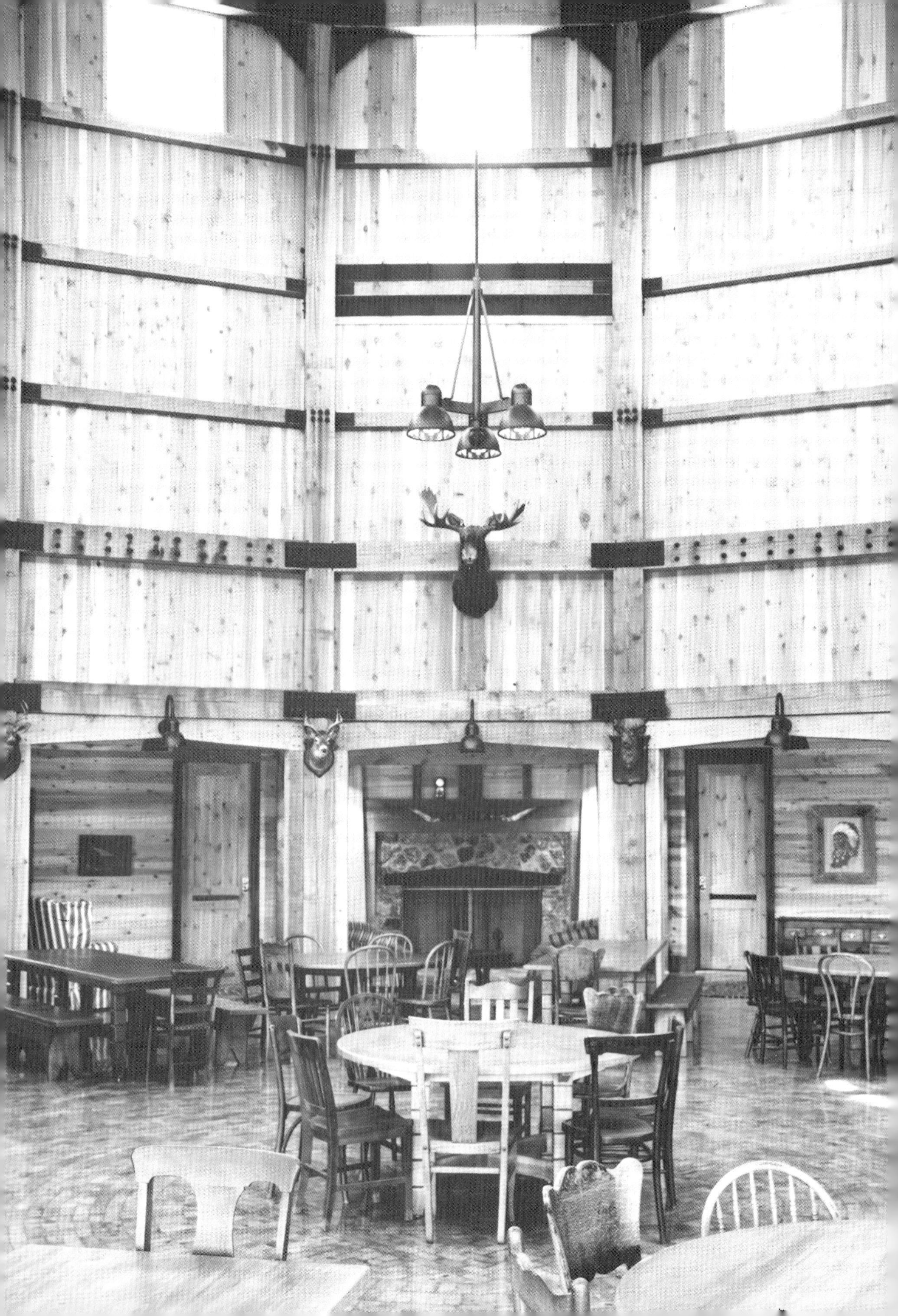

Hole in the Wall Gang Camp
Ashford, Connecticut

Langdon & Woodhouse, Architects, As Interior Design Consultants to Hammond Beeby & Babka, Inc.

Project Team: Tannys Langdon, *Partner in Charge*; Melissa Alderton, Clark Fell, Marsha Woodhouse
Client: Hole in the Wall Gang Camp Fund, Inc.
Buildings Contractor: Konover Construction
Interiors Contractor: Langdon & Woodhouse, Architects
Photographer: Judith Bromley

The Hole in the Wall Gang Camp, a summer camp for children with life-threatening illnesses, was conceived of, developed, and funded as a philanthropic venture by actor Paul Newman. Newman's goal for the camp was to create a place which would look like it had been there forever. He wanted it to be a place where the kids could "raise hell" and avoid the sense of institution. The interiors of the thirty or so buildings are a mixed bag of Americana: custom, reworked, new and found furniture; natural materials, primitive art works; wacky accessories and stenciled walls intended to be both sentimental and silly.

Jury Comments: "Charming... dream project, delicious, has vitality and life... takes a movie set approach and does it very well..."

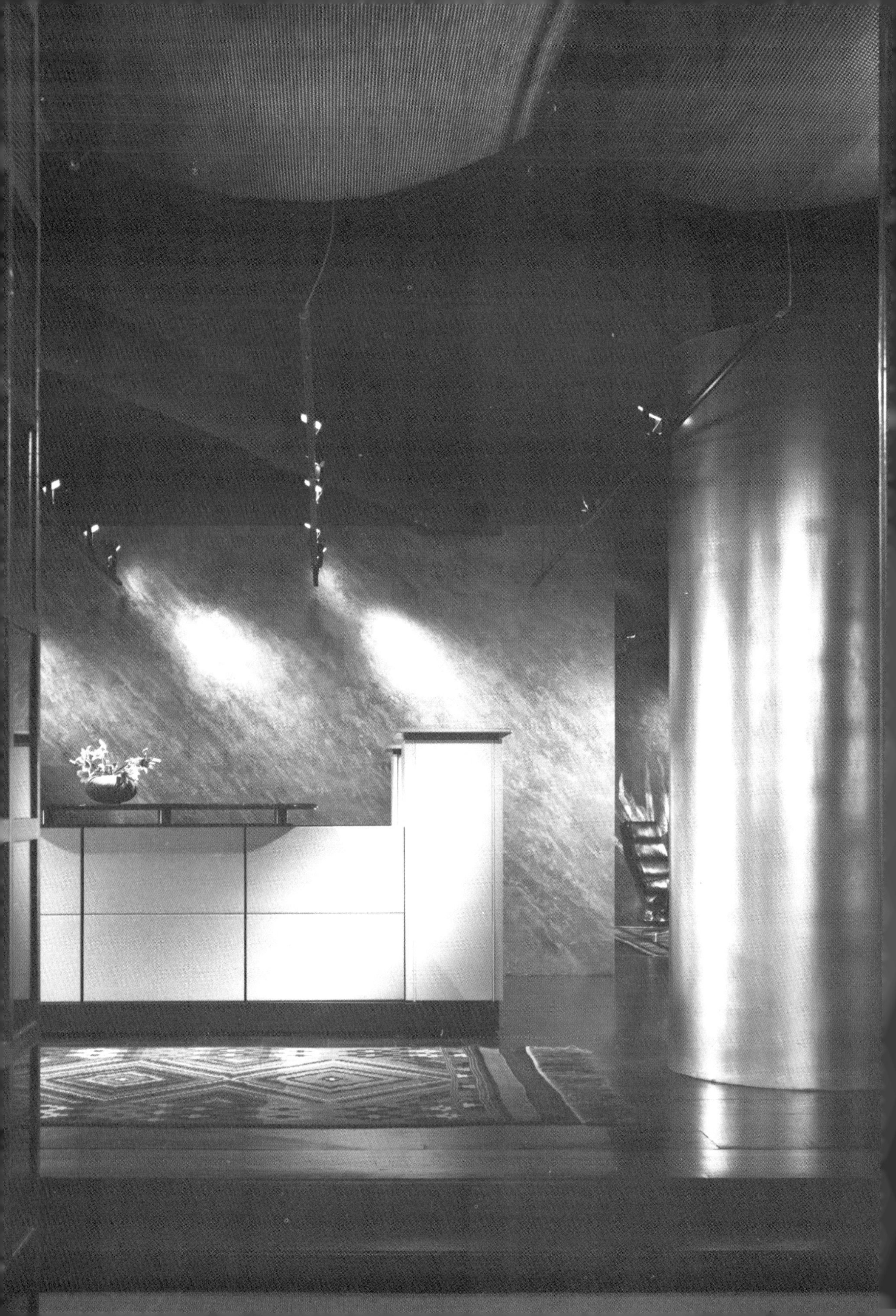

Herman Miller Showroom
Chicago, Illinois

Skidmore, Owings & Merrill

Project Team: Diane Legge, *Design Partner;* William M. Drake, *Project Partner;* Patrick McConnell with Michelle Mirrielees and Carol Hsiung, *Design;* Hal Scheffers, *Technical;* Klaus Mueller, *Project Management*
Client: Herman Miller, Inc.
Contractor: Merchandise Mart Properties
Photographer: Nick Merrick, Hedrich-Blessing

A new showroom presents Herman Miller furniture systems in an atmosphere of visual drama.
The necessary flexibility is provided by a tripartite framework: a raised flooring system houses all electrical, telephone, and computer cables; a hung frame system at ceiling level supports lighting fixtures and fabric-covered panels; and cylindrical cladding encases the structural columns.
The framework also literally sets the stage for the showroom. The stage-like quality of the raised floor is reinforced by the progression of broad pillars which frame the backdrop of the city itself. The partially exposed ceiling creates a soft void, so that all attention is focused on the product areas. The main attractions of the collection are spotlighted from the ceiling frame.

Jury Comments: "Very successful space...striking, seductive...current, interesting use of materials... really took advantage of its location..."

IAA CERTIFICATE OF MERIT

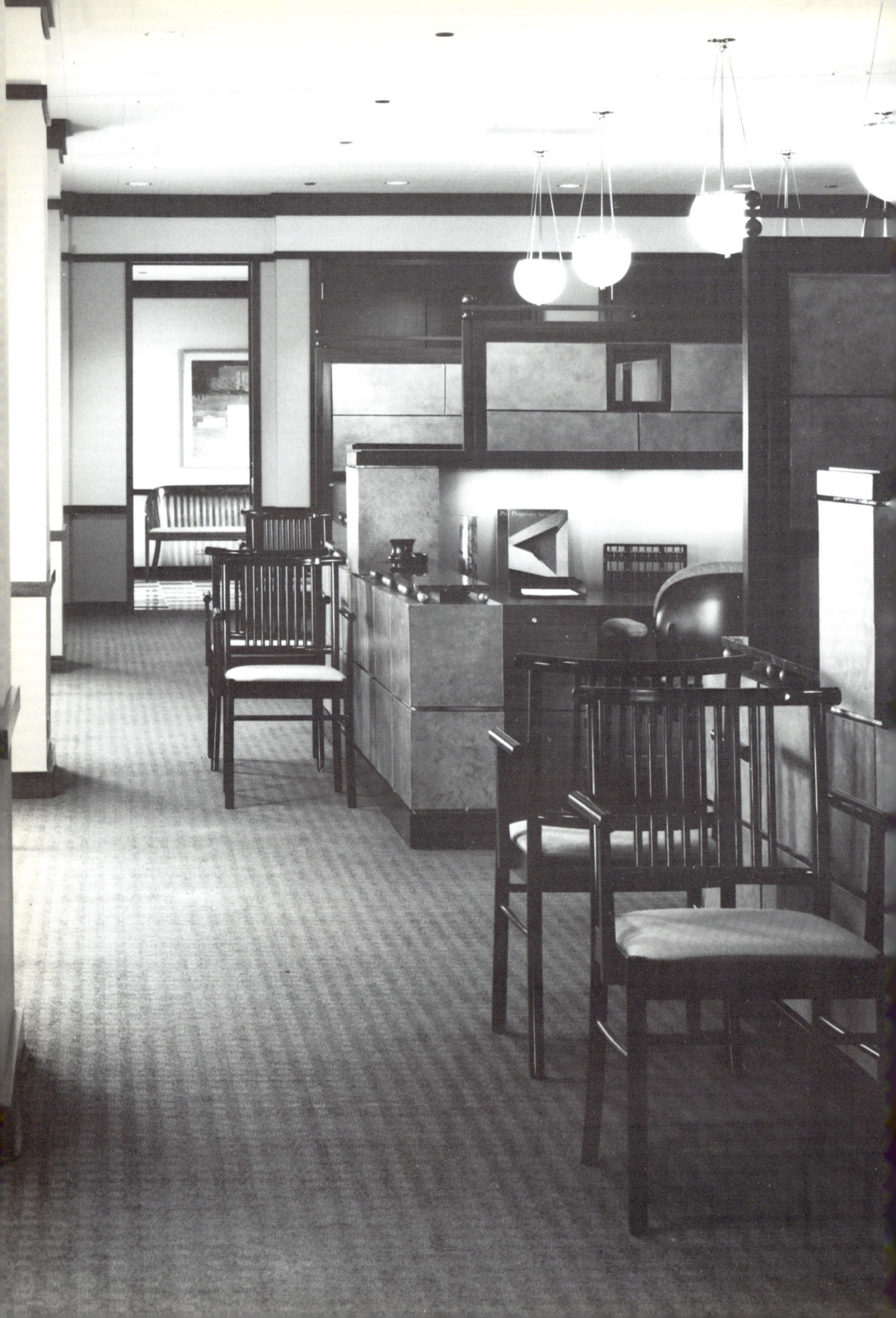

IAA

CERTIFICATE OF MERIT

**Near North Title Company
Chicago, Illinois**

Skidmore, Owings & Merrill

Project Team: Adrian Smith, *Design Partner;* William M. Drake, *Project Partner;* David MacKenzie with Michelle Mirrielees, *Design;* Mark Nelson, *Technical;* Klaus Mueller, *Project Management*
Client: Near North Title Company
Contractor: Ben A. Borenstein & Co.
Specialty Paint Finish: Moore-Tanner
Photographer: Nick Merrick, Hedrich-Blessing

Jury Comments: "Colors are nice... someone gave it a lot of time and effort... brought a nostalgic, very human feel to a space that can be dehumanizing... gave it the charm of 1940s offices..."

A commercial insurance company wished to establish a retail presence in a 7,000-square-foot space adjacent to the lobby of a newly renovated building. A series of windows expose the space to lobby traffic.
The design solution evolved from a careful consideration of the lobby motifs. The varied ceiling height, moving from an intimate low space in the reception area to a grander scale in the work areas, reflects a similar variation in the lobby. Existing mahogany window frames inspire the wood trim which carries a clerestory line throughout the project.
The color scheme is rich, in deep golds and dark grays. Specially designed hanging light fixtures recall the lobby sconces and light fittings.

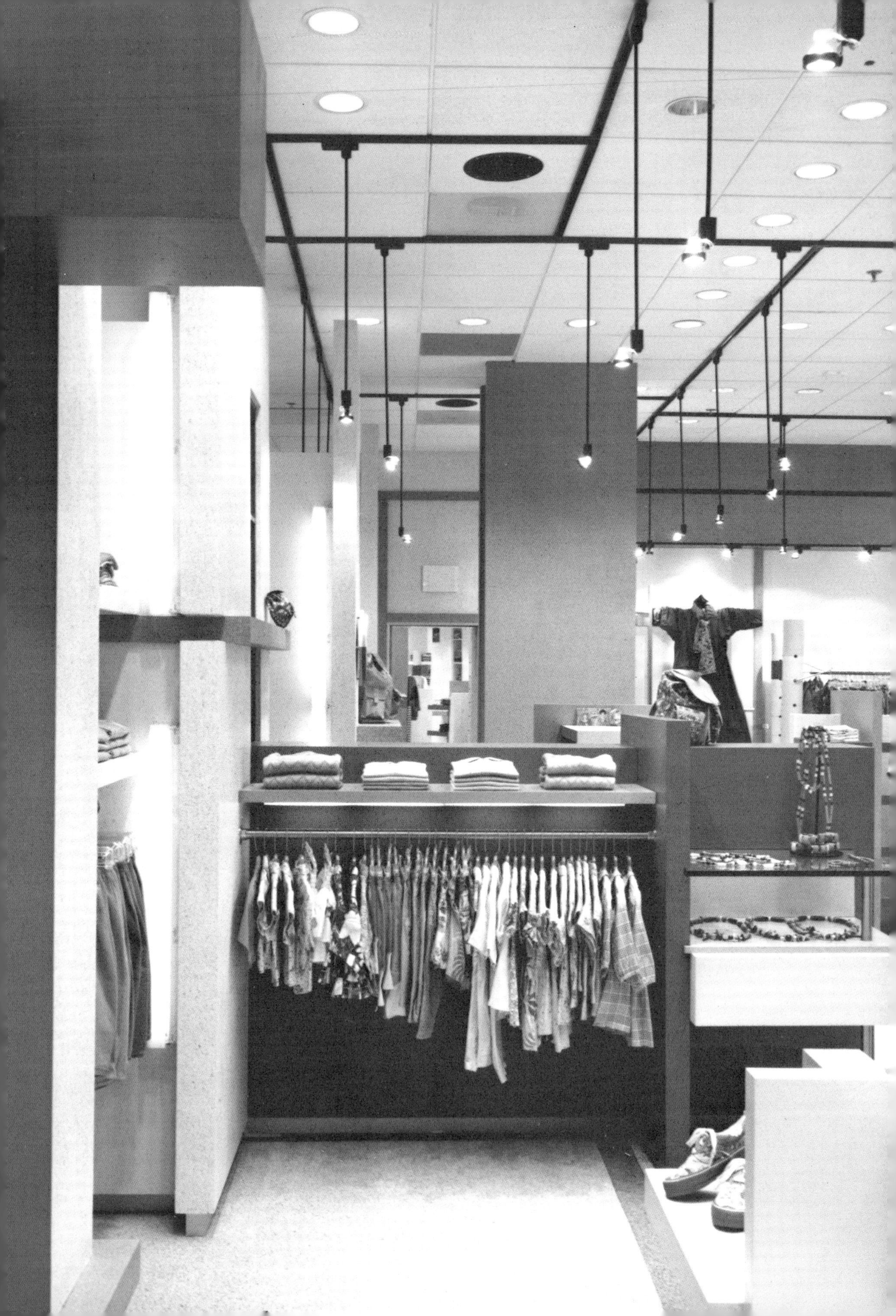

Oilily
Chicago, Illinois

Florian-Wierzbowski Architecture, P.C.

Project Team: Paul Florian, Stephen Wierzbowski, William Worn, *Partners;* Bernadette Planert, *Project Architect;* Jeff S. Henriksen, *Delineator*
Client: Oilily/Chicago
Contractor: C.D. Build Group, Ltd.
Mechanical Engineer: Cosentini
Structural Engineer: Howard Stearn
Lighting: Chicago Lighting
Graphic Design: Michael Glass Design
Photographer: Wayne Cable

A colorful constructivist environment houses a store for women and children's clothing from Holland. Abstract de Stijl forms suggest that the clothing is modern, "artful," and Dutch. Vertical and horizontal lighting patterns complement the floor patterns and dressing platforms. The painted display tables are divided to explain clothing ensembles. Both tables and walls appear to have left traces of movement in the floor pattern. Freestanding pole display fixtures and a stabilized gravel floor contribute to a free-spirited and playful atmosphere.

***Jury Comments:** "Color and geometric forms are fresh, attractive... fun, engaging space... doesn't overtake merchandise, enhances it... children would like it..."*

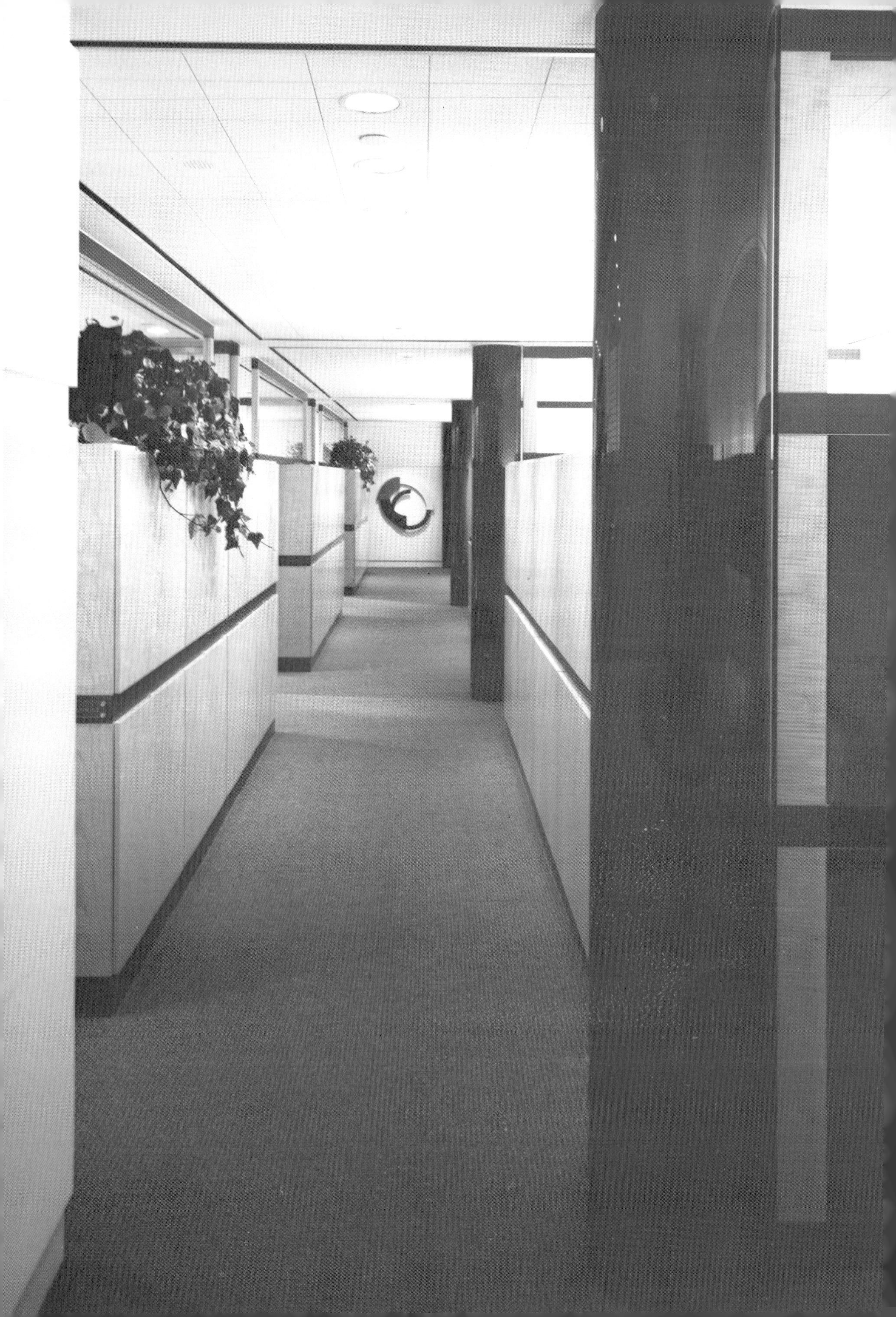

IAA

Certificate of Merit

**Woodwork Corporation of America
Chicago, Illinois**

Powell/Kleinschmidt, Inc.

Project Team: Robert D. Kleinschmidt, Donald Los, William Arnold, Thomas Boeman, Emily Berlinghof and Donna Rasinski
Client: Woodwork Corporation of America
Contractor: Woodwork Corporation of America
Engineer: Mid-Continent Engineering, Inc.
Photographer: Jon Miller, Hedrich-Blessing

These refurbished offices convey the strong sense of craft and expert capabilities of the client, the largest custom millwork manufacturer in the Midwest.

The architects used a choice combination of different woods and finishes, ranging from both hand-rubbed and open-pore lacquer to high-gloss polyester, stained particle board, and marquetry. A matrix of French white ash paneling and American cherry banding defines clerestories and open and closed spaces.

Other design elements include columns clad in high-gloss polyester and built-in seating in the reception area. Warm incandescent ceiling lights compliment the tones and textures of the various woods. The art program is entirely composed of pieces made of or referring to wood.

Jury Comments: "Good job... incorporates sleek image design and detailing into factory setting..."

10
TE
YEA
AWAR

This year, the Interior Architecture Committee commemorates ten years of recognizing outstanding design in this unique discipline by establishing the Ten Year Award. Projects for the Ten Year Award were judged based on their exceptional significance and lasting value to the interior architecture profession. The Ten Year Award recipients were chosen from the collected winners of the past nine years as well as the 1989 award recipients.

Banco de Occidente
Guatemala City, Guatemala

Skidmore, Owings & Merrill

Jury Comments: *"You can feel its presence; it's timeless... sensitive courtyard ... use of color is really quite wonderful ... major design statement... just a beautiful project, incorporates the inside, the outside, the street... a series of different spaces are well integrated... very complete project..."*

Local materials, architectural concepts, and construction materials were used throughout these three buildings for one of the oldest banking institutions in Guatemala. Concrete and concrete block faced with stucco, small volcanic stone pavers, local mahogany, local fabrics and locally available glass are the predominant materials.

Open courtyards, terraces, gardens, fountains, and trellises reinforce the buildings' relationship to the native context. Large pivoting mahogany doors and operable wood louvers allow air to circulate. Because each site is subject to frequent power failures, the buildings can and do function at times without artificial light and power.

Project Team: Bruce J. Graham, *Design* and *Project Partner*; Adrian D. Smith, *Design Partner*; Patrick McConnell, *Design*
Client: Banco de Occidente
Contractor: Holzheu y Hernandez Asociados
Photographer: Nick Wheeler

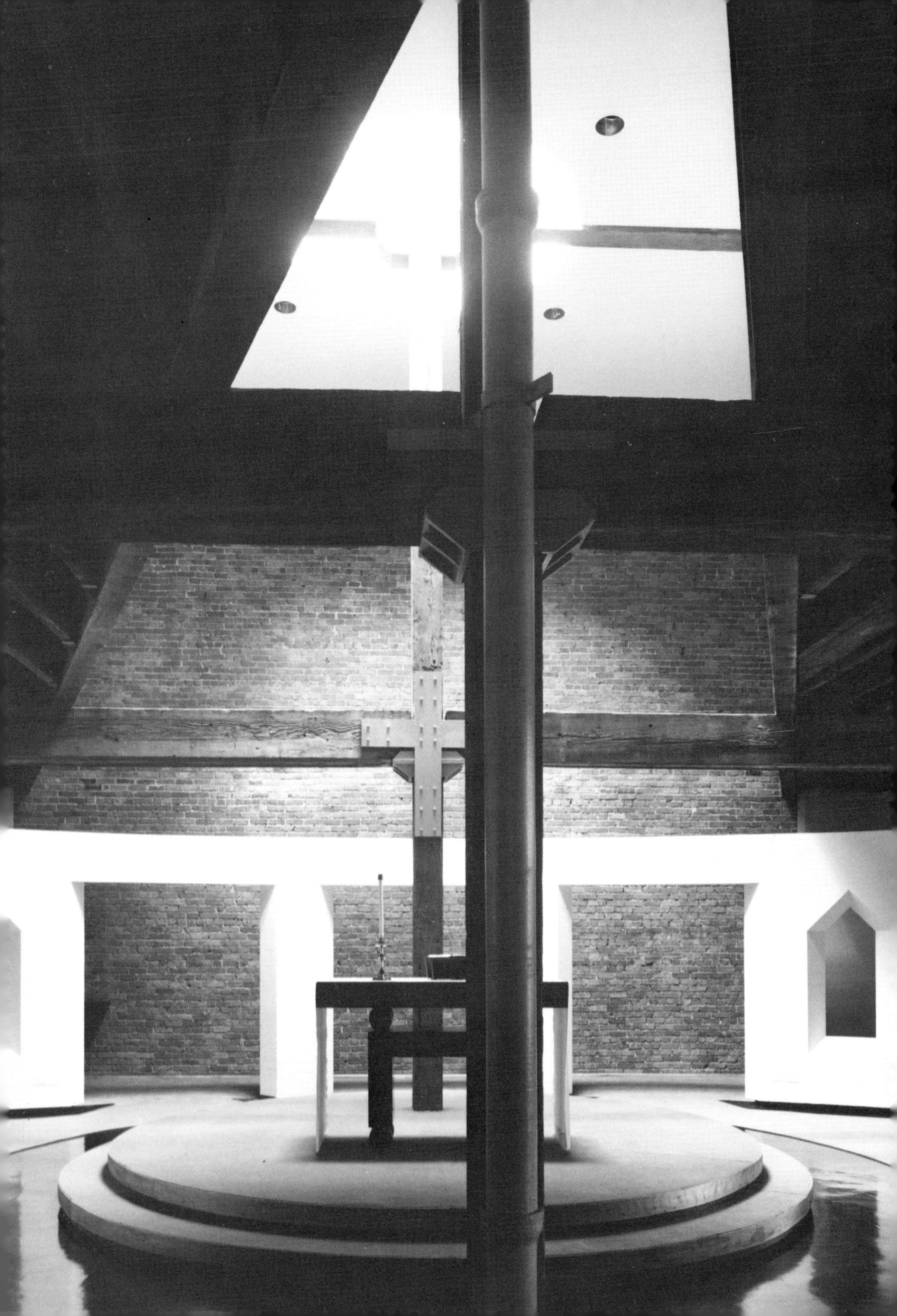

IAA

TEN YEAR AWARD

**Grace Place Episcopal
Church and Community Center
Chicago, Illinois**

Booth/Hansen & Associates

Project Team: Laurence Booth, *Design Principal;* Paul Hansen, *Managing Principal;* Laura Weyrauch, *Managing Architect;* Richard Merrifield
Client: Grace Episcopal Church
Contractor: W. B. Olson, Inc.
Structural Engineer: Beer, Gorski & Graff
Electrical Engineer: Nixon Electrical
HVAC Engineer: Westside Mechanical
Plumbing: Leonard V. Stutz & Sons
Photographer: Timothy Hursley/The Arkansas Office

Jury Comments: "Very much in the spirit of Chicago--a community effort. . . you can feel the presence of the client, the congregation. . . straight-forward architectural contributions which create a place for worship . . . has a certain handmade quality about it. . . not overdone. . . very simple, very strong. . ."

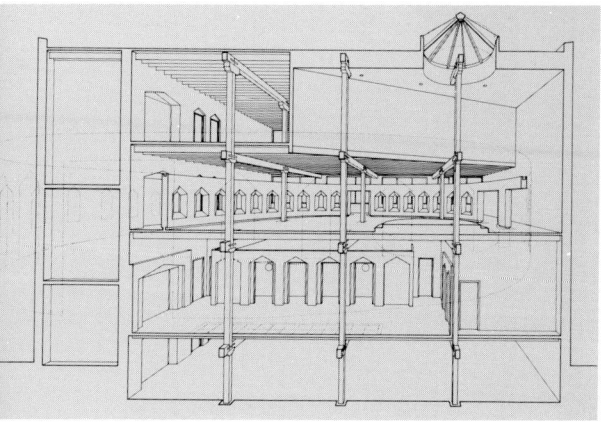

Grace Episcopal Church occupies a three-story heavy timber and masonry structure in an urban redevelopment area of rehabbed loft buildings and new townhouses. A street-level community center provides facilities for neighborhood gatherings, meetings, and exhibits.
The second-floor sanctuary is the heart of the building. Placed within the framework of the secular grid, the spirited form of an elliptical wall encloses the sacred space within. Arched windows in the wall allow light from large exterior windows to filter into the sanctuary. Over a circular altar platform, a triangular section of the floor above has been removed, and a skylight sheds light on the altar below.

153

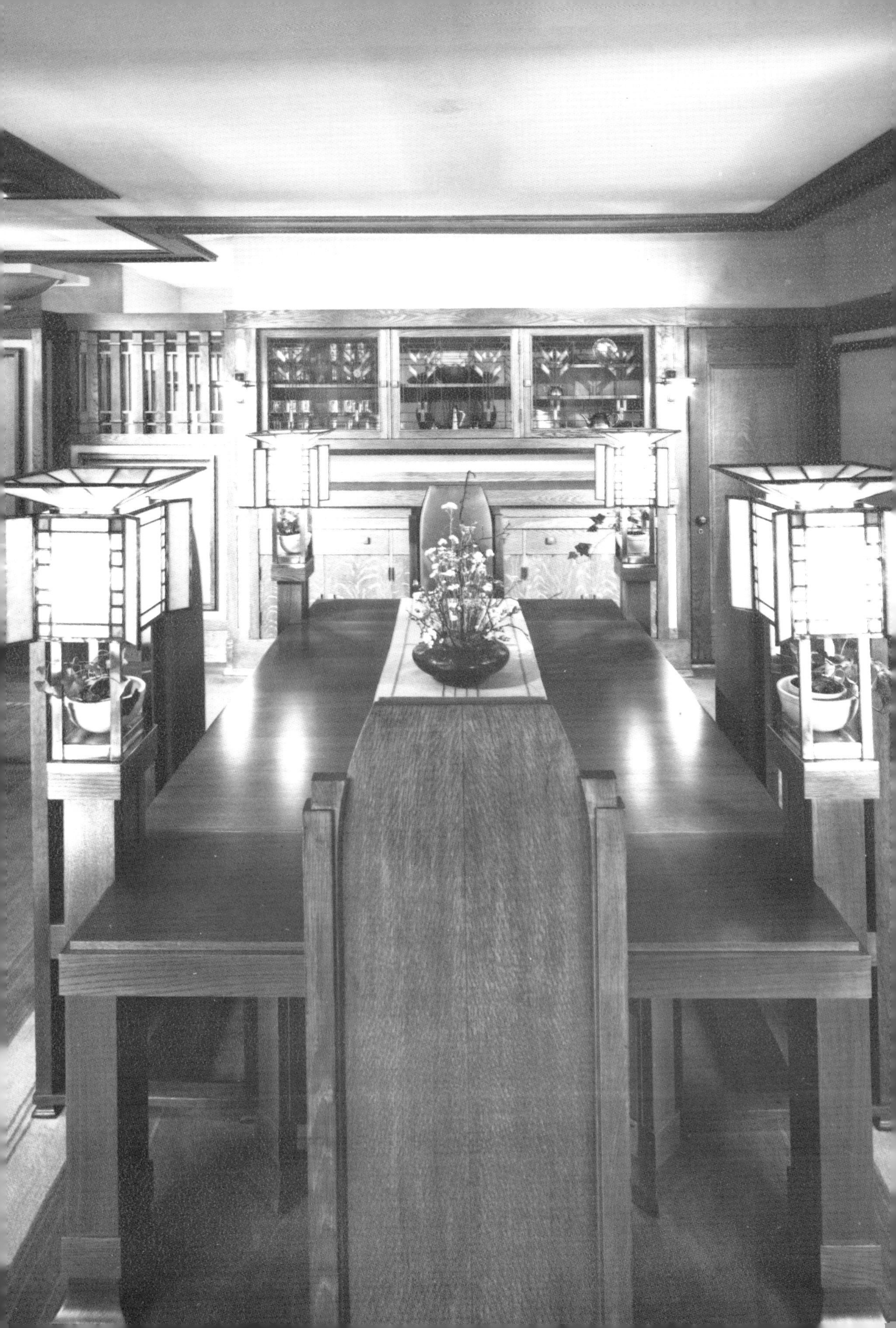

Meyer May House Museum
Grand Rapids, Michigan

Tilton + Lewis Associates, Inc.

Jury Comments: "They really went out of their way. . . deepens the concept of restoration in the best sense. . . the thoroughness of the project was rewarding. . . wonderful to give that kind of care to bring back an old beauty. . . lasting so that others can enjoy it. . . applause to the client for vision and commitment. . ."

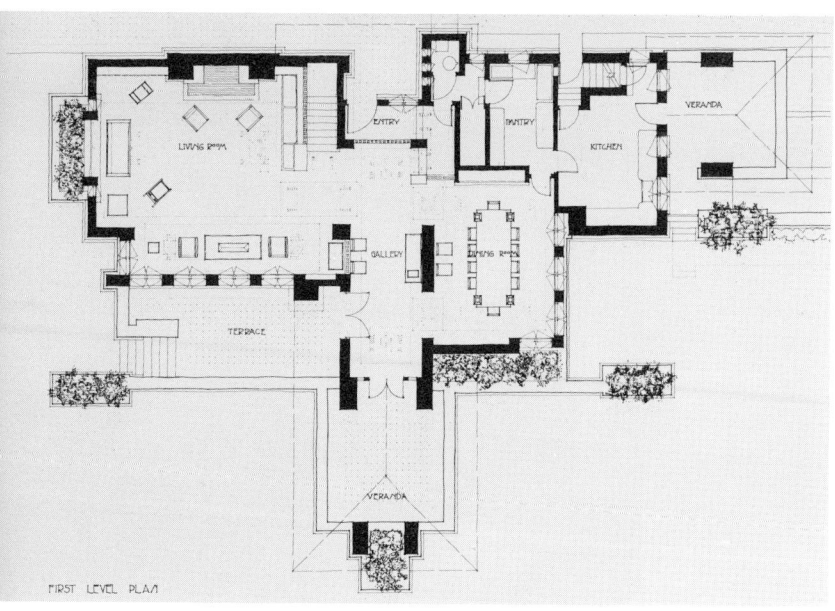

An extensive search for documentation and original furnishings was undertaken to reconstruct the interiors of this 1909 Frank Lloyd Wright design. The HVAC system concealed in the basement and attic provides a controlled environment for original furnishings which were purchased and reconditioned to museum quality for the house. Historic photographs and sketches were consulted to aid in the re-creation of the missing furniture.

The 1909 color schemes were replicated with paint and wood finish analysis. The original designs and yarn samples aided in the reproduction of the carpets.

Project Team: Carla Lind, *Steelcase Project Director;* David Hanks, *Decorative Arts Consultant;* Tim Hofstra
Client: Steelcase, Inc.
Contractor: Barnes Construction Company
Photographer: Jon Miller, Hedrich-Blessing

DDA

DIVIN
DETAIL
AWARD

DDA

The Divine Detail Award was initiated in 1989 to recognize instances where the expression of architectural theory becomes an artistic medium, defining the relationship between architecture and craft. Projects should illustrate the governing design concept of the building through the use of a particular material, detail, or technology. Both new and adaptive re-use projects completed between January 1, 1986 and May 1, 1989 are eligible. Projects must be designed by registered architects with offices in the Chicago metropolitan area. The jury is chosen by the Design Committee.

JURY DDA

Clockwise from top left:
John F. Hartray, Jr., FAIA
Nagle, Hartray & Associates, Ltd.

Gerald Horn, FAIA
Holabird & Root

Christopher Rudolph, AIA
Rudolph & Associates, P.C.

DDA SUBMISSIONS

▼
Buchanan Residence
Peter Landon Architects, Ltd.
Photo: Peter Landon

▶
Bond Brewing/ G. Heileman Brewing USA
J. Torchia Associates
Photo: James Yochum

▼
Chicago Greystone
by Monice Malnar, AIA
Photo: Frank J. Jodvarka

◀
Chapel for Church of the Annunciata
Harding Associates
Photo: Bruce Van Inwegen

159

DDA SUBMISSIONS

▲
Commerce Plaza Entrance Pavilion
Jack Train Associates, Inc.
Photo: Jack Train Associates, Inc.

▼
Just Wonderful Stuff
Environ, Inc.
Photo: Terry Lee

▲
Country Estate
Decker and Kemp
Photo: Mark Heffron

▶
Lally Residence
Serena-Sturm Architects, Ltd.
Photo: Serena-Sturm Architects, Ltd.

DDA SUBMISSIONS

▼
O'Hare Airport Mail Facility
Booth/Hansen & Associates, Ltd.
Photo: Steinkamp/Ballogg

▲
MetroWest Office Building Management and Leasing Offices
Jack Train Associates, Inc.
Photo: Jack Train Associates, Inc.

◄
One Conway Park
Booth/Hansen & Associates, Ltd.
Photo: Randy Hafer

◄
Pansophic Systems, Inc., World Headquarters
F.I. Torchia Associates
Photo: James Yochum

161

DDA SUBMISSIONS

◄
Sieben's River North Brewery
Wallace Bowling Architects
Photo: Julie Myers

◄
Stremmel House
Riverside Architects
Photo: Howard N. Kaplan
▼
Sukkah at North Shore Congregation Israel  
John Syvertsen
Photo: Howard N. Kaplan

▲
Rowes Wharf
Skidmore, Owings & Merrill
Photo: Steve Rosenthal
▶
Tech Two Lobby
Michael J. Pado AIA Architect, Ltd.
Photo: Michael J. Pado

DDA SUBMISSIONS

▶
Willow Lake Centre
Harry Weese & Associates
Photo: Hedrich-Blessing and HWA

Townhouse Remodeling
Quinn and Searl, Architects
Photo: George Lambros

United Gulf Bank Sun Screens
Skidmore, Owings & Merrill
Photo: Nick Merrick, Hedrich-Blessing

▲
United Gulf Bank Glass Block Atrium
Skidmore, Owings & Merrill
Photo: Nick Merrick, Hedrich-Blessing
◀
303 West Madison
Skidmore, Owings & Merrill
Photo: Hedrich-Blessing

HONOR AWARD DDA

United Gulf Bank
Manama, Bahrain

Skidmore, Owings & Merrill

Jury Comments: "Everything you could want technically... you get the feeling they've been doing this for 200 years... fits into the facade... you couldn't pull it out, integral to the design..."

The screen-like expression of this bank's facade is a modern interpretation of the *mushrabiyya*, the traditional Islamic sunscreen. Like the *mushrabiyya*, the sun control system provides daylight without heat or glare and affords views without sacrificing privacy. Natural daylight is diffused by a glass transom.

A fiberglass light shelf reflects the diffused light upward across the coved ceiling. This light shelf also prevents high southern sunlight from entering the room directly, while diagonal green glass fins reduce solar penetration from low western sunlight without obstructing views from within. Clear reflective insulating glass further reduces solar gain. Natural light is thus transformed from a hot, harsh force of nature into a pleasant interior light source.

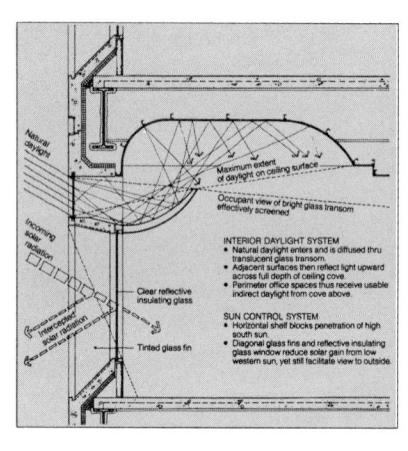

Client: United Gulf Bank
Contractor: Shimizu Construction Company, Ltd.
Structural Engineer: Skidmore, Owings & Merrill
Mechanical/Electrical Engineer: Pan Arab Consulting Engineers
Photographer: Nick Merrick, Hedrich-Blessing

DDA CERTIFICATE OF MERIT

**Buchanan Residence
Peter Landon Architects Ltd.**

Northfield, Illinois

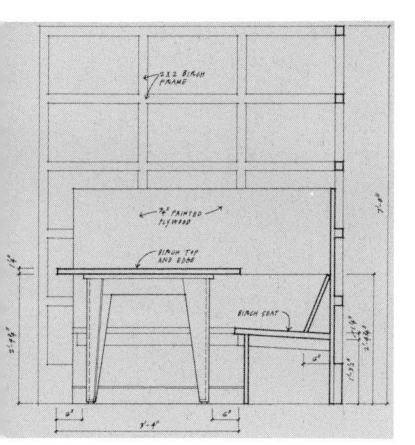

A mid-1960s suburban split-level is expanded with a series of sculptural spaces at the rear of the house. The addition opens off the kitchen at a built-in breakfast niche. The bench and its lattice frame form an L-shaped screen which partially encloses the kitchen. Similar materials, colors, and finishes integrate the two spaces. Table, bench, and chairs are all built of birch veneer plywood.
Project Team: Peter Landon, Malcolm Edgerton, Norah Edelstein
Client: Drs. Robert and Ellen Buchanan
Contractor: Teschky, Inc.
Furniture Craftsman: Jim Moratto
Photographer: Peter Landon, Wayne Cable/Cable Studies

Jury Comments: "Doing the Lord's work... inexpensive but done very carefully, a great deal of thought given to how joints were made... another aesthetic for plywood.. fits together with integrity... well thought out..."

DDA

CERTIFICATE OF MERIT

**Commerce Plaza Entrance Pavilion
Oak Brook, Illinois**

Jack Train Associates, Inc.

Jury Comments: "Craftsmanship is unbelievable... takes the OSHA standard a couple of steps beyond... sophisticated, very elegant... good thinking about the smaller elements of a building...

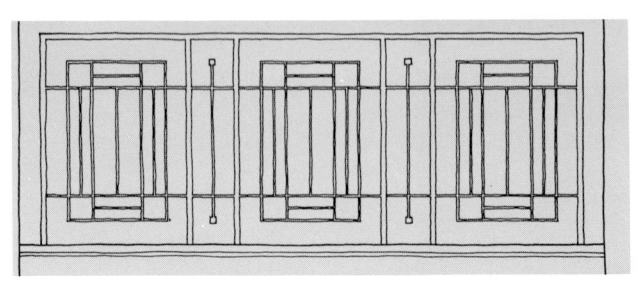

Polished stainless steel rails and window grillwork in this office complex entrance pavilion reflect motifs used in the building's precast concrete and granite cladding. The reflective and tactile qualities of hand-polished stainless steel encourage people to touch and examine at close range the carefully crafted railings.
Client: Metropolitan Life Insurance Company
Structural Engineer: Don Belford Associates
Mechanical/Electrical Engineer: Environmental Systems Design
Photographer: Jack Train Associates, Inc.

166

DDA CERTIFICATE OF MERIT

**Just Wonderful Stuff
Chicago, Illinois**

Environ, Inc.

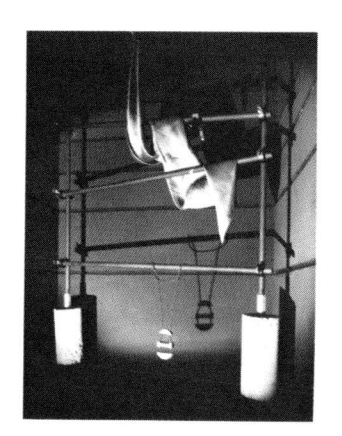

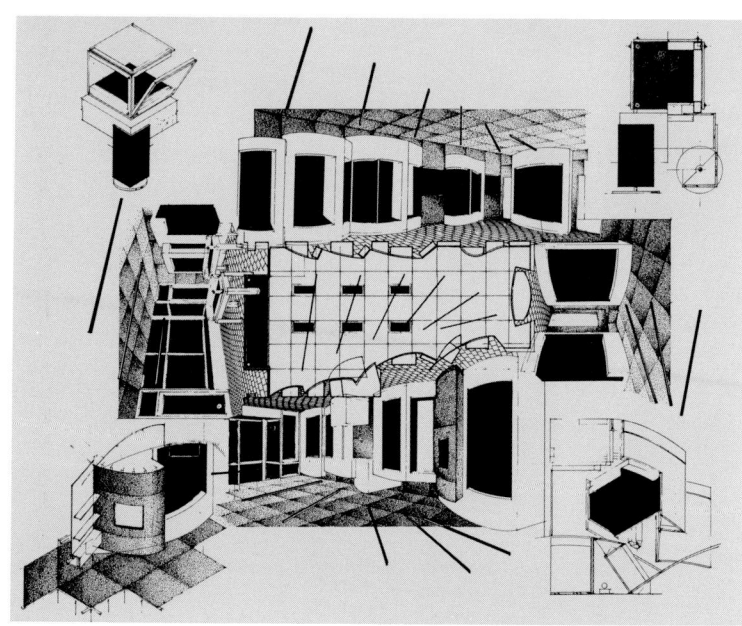

This retail space is set within a shell of perforated raw metal ceiling panels and walls. A series of display units frame merchandise with an arch evoking a theatre proscenium. Island display cases are simple crystalline boxes of glass and polished metal. They rest on raw metal bases with painted steel legs and levelers. In both boxes and proscenium units, a background of flat black rubber mats sets off the vivid colors of the merchandise.

The mounted hanging display unit consists of vertical gunmetal finish rods with concrete stabilizing weights. Crossbars and adjustable fittings assure maximum flexibility for changing displays.

Project Team: John H. Nelson, AIA; Bradley Schenkel
Client: Barbara Moss
Contractor: Miller Construction Company
Photographer: Terry Lee

Jury Comments: "Nice to know when to stop-- absence of a lot of show window hardware...lighting handled well, focuses all attention on merchandise ...hard to pinpoint which detail is the best part..."

25
TWENTY-FIVE YEAR AWARD

25

The Chicago Chapter AIA Twenty-Five Year Awards program was initiated in 1979 to recognize significant projects twenty-five years after their completion. CCAIA Distinguished Building Award Winners from the relevant years are automatically eligible for nomination. Projects must be designed by a registered architect who may be based anywhere in the world. The Historic Resources Committee selects the jury, which reviews the submissions using both contemporary and vintage photos.

JURY & STATEMENT

The 1989 jury devoted much discussion to the response of each design to its physical setting. Site issues became an important criterion for evaluation of the entries. These issues were addressed in terms of both their architectural context and natural environment.

Each building was considered for both its individual design and the degree to which it represents an architectural type. The question was raised whether it was proper to celebrate the most fitting example of the evolution of the architectural type that "breaks the mold".

The jury noted the "revisionist" quality of looking back at and interpreting the architecture of twenty-five years ago. This kind of historical perspective allows a second look at buildings that were not adequately appreciated in the past, as well as a re-evaluation of those already recognized.

A building designed by a Chicago-area firm but constructed outside of Chicago was selected for the 1989 CCAIA Twenty-Five Year Award. The jury noted that it is the purpose of the chapter to support the work of its professional membership, regardless of where the project is located.

Finally, the jury expressed its conviction that the work of twenty-five years ago is of great interest to today's architectural community and deserves further examination.

Clockwise from top left:
Kevin Harrington
Associate Professor of Architectural History, Illinois Institute of Technology

Judith S. Hull
Assistant Professor, History of Architecture and Art Department, University of Illinois at Chicago

Anders Nereim, AIA
Architect in private practice, Chicago
Visiting editor, *Inland Architect*

TWENTY-FIVE YEAR AWARD RECIPIENT

**First Baptist Church
Columbus, Indiana**

Harry Weese & Associates

*Jury Comments:
"Extremely interesting, very resonant... strong calligraphy of silhouette... wonderfully sited in the shallow hill, floats there in the context of no context... gives definition to its suburban site and coherence to its neighborhood... Weese successfully pays homage to his teacher Saarinen and the First Christian Church..."*

At the First Baptist Church, a number of functions are contained in a unified grouping of simple forms associated with traditional church architecture. The building, sited atop a rolling hill, integrates functional and educational requirements, permitting worship spaces to dominate the ensemble.
The sanctuary, chapel, community hall, small kitchen, and pastor's office are on the upper floor, while the lower floor consists of classrooms. The interior spaces face a central courtyard which provides a fair-weather classroom and meditation area. The building is constructed with a concrete floor and exposed brick-bearing walls. The roof is made of heavy timber covered with green Vermont slate.
The sanctuary seats 500 on both sides of a non-symmetrical aisle which focuses on the communion table and cross. A brick wall screens the choir, organ, and baptistery from the congregation. Natural ventilation and simple finishes emphasize form rather than material.

Harry Weese & Associates
Completion Date: 1965
Contractor: Repp & Mundt
Photographer: Balthazar Korab

DSA

DISTINGUISHED

SERVICE

AWARDS

DSA

The Chicago Chapter AIA Distinguished Service Award recognizes outstanding service to the Chicago architectural community. The award may be given both to individuals and organizations; it may be given for a body of work or for a specific project. Past winners have included photographers, craftsmen, educators, authors, institutions, and architects. Nominations are made by Chicago Chapter members. The CCAIA Board of Directors reviews and votes on the nominations.

RECIPIENT DSA

Leon M. Despres

Leon Despres, former 5th ward Alderman, former City Council Parliamentarian, former member of the Chicago Plan Commission, practicing attorney, outspoken advocate of the disenfranchised and neglected in our community, is a Chicago legend. Mr. Despres, whose independent and articulate voice has been so clearly heard for many decades, has spent much of his time and energy exhorting Chicagoans, and especially Chicago's elected leadership, to make our city a well-planned, compassionate, and responsive place in which to live and work.

Graduating from the Law School and the University of Chicago in 1929, Mr. Despres began a long and distinguished career in labor law and issues related to civil rights. Elected as the very independent alderman of the 5th ward in 1955, Mr. Despres consistently represented integrity and fairness in the City Council during a period when these qualities were so repeatedly absent. Often a lone and creative city legislator working against overwhelming political odds, Mr. Despres nonetheless is credited with the creation of the Municipal Housing Code, the Chicago Planning Commission, and the Chicago Commission on Historic and Architectural Landmarks.

Mr. Despres has worked tirelessly to defend the city's lakefront–and in fact all areas of Chicago–against the threat of over-development. As a ten-year member of the Planning Commission, he argued in favor of controlled density. He advocated city planning efforts that considered more than the individual developments themselves, but which also were concerned with the impact on the neighbors and

Top: Leon Despres' mobile office, circa 1961
Below: Leon Despres, moderating a Bughouse Square debate

DSA RECIPIENT

Left: Mr. Despres, speaking at a community meeting at the Church of the Disciples
Below: Dedicating a statue of LaSalle on May 1, 1981

the adjacent streets. In addition, he championed a development and planning review process that would be open and fair.

Throughout his career in public life, Mr. Despres has felt that "the creation of a creative and workable urban plan, to replace the city's planless growth and exploitation...was the key to obtaining constructive urban renewal, rational housing programs, correction of slums, neighborhood maintenance, and prevention of decay." It is this legacy of thoughtful leadership and Distinguished Service to the public that stands as a beacon for those who work to make our city--and all cities--a balanced, just, and civilized community.

DSA RECIPIENT

John F. Hartray, Jr., FAIA

Mr. Hartray, a native of the Chicago area, has long been one of the AIA's most active and influential participants. Graduating with his Bachelor of Architecture from Cornell in 1954, Mr. Hartray returned to practice in Chicago, becoming Project Manager of Harry Weese and Associates in 1961 and Executive Vice-President in 1965. In 1977, he became a Principal in the firm of Booth, Nagle and Hartray, which divided in 1980; he is now a Principal in the firm of Nagle, Hartray and Associates.

During his tenure with Harry Weese and Associates, Mr. Hartray managed projects which included the remodeling of the Newberry Library, the restoration of Louis Sullivan's Auditorium Theatre, the Time & Life Building in Chicago, and the Campbell Correctional Center. Mr. Hartray also established all of the management systems used during the course of the Washington, D.C. Metro subway system.

While with Mr. Nagle at Nagle, Hartray and Associates, Mr. Hartray has been involved with managerial and technical aspects in the full range of the firm's projects, some of which include a 50-story apartment structure under construction in Chicago, a new downtown Terminal Building for the Greyhound Bus Company, a major corporate office campus in Memphis, Tennessee, the Ramada Renaissance Hotel in Springfield, Illinois, and a host of other residential, institutional, and corporate assignments.

Mr. Hartray's involvement in public service activities is extensive: his contributions to the life of his community and his profession are an example to all of his colleagues. He has been especially concerned about the training and licensing of architects: he served on the

Top: Perspective for the Chicago Greyhound Bus Terminal
Below: John F. Hartray, Jr., FAIA

176

DSA RECIPIENT

National Architectural Accreditation Board from 1977-1979, making many visits to collegiate schools of Architecture across the country. He has taught architecture widely, and is currently an Adjunct Professor of Architecture at the University of Illinois at Chicago and the Illinois Institute of Technology.

He has served on the Board of Directors of both the Chicago Chapter and the National AIA. He chaired the AIA National Commission on Design in 1975 and served on the AIA Task Force for the design of the National Capitol Master Plan. He was a member of the architectural task force sponsored by the National Science Foundation to study and report on the results of the 1976 earthquake in Guatemala. He has served on several Mayor's Committees in Chicago, looking at a range of issues including planning and zoning: Mr. Hartray is one of the city's leading experts on zoning matters. He is also a founding member of ADPSR–Architects, Designers, and Planners for Social Responsibility–and is a Board member of the Chicago Chapter.

As a writer, Mr. Hartray contributed a regular column for the AIA's publication, *Architectural Technology*, entitled "Low Tech." He has contributed articles to all of the national and local journals on architecture, and has also written for Chicago's daily newspapers.

Mr. Hartray was made a Fellow of the AIA in 1979, and has acted as teacher, mentor, and model to all of his fellow professionals. His has been a truly Distinguished Service to his profession.

Left: Greyhound Terminal under construction
Below: Illustration drawn by Mr. Hartray for an article in the CCAIA *Focus*

YAA

YOUNG
ARCHITECT
AWARD

YAA

The Chicago Chapter AIA Young Architect Award was established in 1981 to recognize superior achievement and outstanding promise in young architects. Eligible candidates must be between the ages of twenty-five and thirty-nine on September 9, 1989. Nominations are made either by Chicago Chapter AIA members or by the individuals themselves. The nominee does not have to be an AIA member, nor a registered architect. The Design Committee selects the jury.

JURY YAA

Clockwise from top left:
John Syvertsen, AIA
John Syvertsen Architect

Walter Netsch, FAIA
Retired Partner, SOM

Steve Weiss, AIA
Solomon Cordwell Buenz & Associates, Inc.
President, Chicago Chapter AIA

YAA RECIPIENT

Dennis E. Rupert, AIA

Dennis Rupert is a principal with Hammond Beeby and Babka, where he has worked since 1979. He received a Bachelor of Architecture degree from the Illinois Institute of Technology and was a visiting scholar in classical studies at Temple University abroad in Rome. His design experience includes residences, housing, museums, commercial and renovation projects. As principal-in-charge, he has personally directed the project team on jobs of such scope as the Rice Building at the Art Institute of Chicago, the renovation of Eleven South LaSalle and the Phoenix Municipal Government Center competition. He has been the project architect or co-principal-in-charge on such projects as North Shore Congregation Israel and the Harold Washington Library Center. Current work includes the Toledo Museum of Art Master Plan and Renovation, the competition for the completion of the Federal Triangle in Washington, D.C., and a private residence in New Mexico.

Left: Daniel F. and Ada L. Rice Pavilion, Art Institute of Chicago
Below: Dennis E. Rupert, AIA

He has participated in lectures, juries, and symposia at various institutions, including a number of midwestern universities, the Chicago Historical Society, the Art Institute of Chicago, the Chicago Architectural Club and the Chicago Architecture Foundation. Articles he has authored have been published in *Threshold* and *Architectural Design*.

The work of Hammond Beeby and Babka has received national and international recognition through exhibits, publications, and awards. Projects in which Mr. Rupert has had direct involvement have been exhibited in the

U.S., Spain, Italy, and Japan and have appeared in design journals such as *Inland Architect*, *A + U* (Japan), *Progressive Architecture*, and *Architectural Design*.

Project awards include a 1984 National Honor Award from the American Institute of Architects for North Shore Congregation Israel; a Neocon Honor Award in 1988 for the Formica Showroom in Chicago; and a 1988 citation in the *Progressive Architecture* National Design Awards program for the Harold Washington Library Center in Chicago.

Throughout all of Mr. Rupert's works, the 1989 Young Architects Award Jury felt in their review that he has clearly demonstrated the ability to develop conceptual designs into distinguished finished projects.

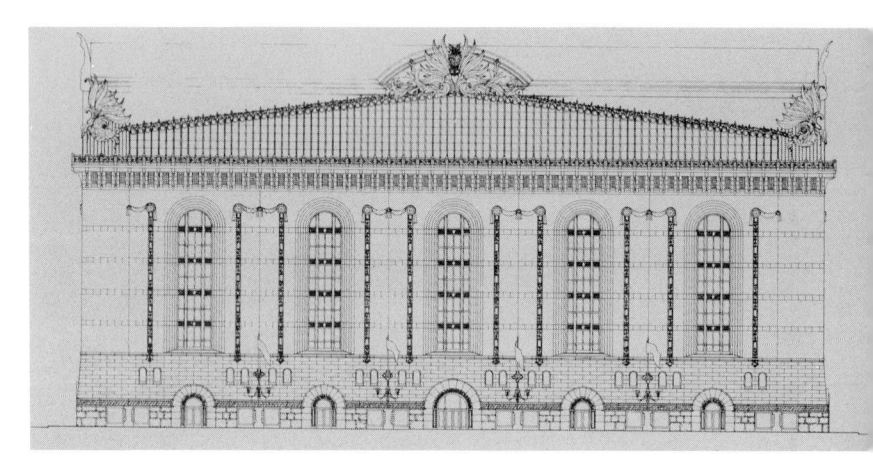

Above: Harold Washington Library Center

CHICAGO AWARD

The Chicago Award was initiated in 1983 to recognize outstanding student work from six regional architecture schools: the University of Illinois at Chicago, the University of Illinois at Champaign, the Illinois Institute of Technology, the University of Notre Dame, the University of Michigan, and the University of Wisconsin - Milwaukee. Each school can select and submit up to ten projects completed during the 1988-1989 school year. From the winners, the jury selects the recipient of the $500 Benn/Johnck Award, which was established in 1984 by William Benn, AIA, to honor his late partner, Frederick Johnck, AIA. An exhibit of the winning projects will appear at the Chicago Historical Society.

JURY & STATEMENT

CA

Although fewer entries were submitted than in previous years, the abundance of accomplished works made the selection of this year's Chicago Award winners difficult. Many projects exhibited arresting designs and beautiful renderings. A number of entries revealed successful solutions to complex programs and provocative problems. The best works demonstrated a rational design process at work, yielding a fully developed idea of great clarity.

The projects chosen for the Award display all the above qualities, and yet go a step further. They are distinguished by their shared ability to deliver a powerful, memorable image–an image which succeeds in evoking a mood appropriate for the scale of the project and the essence of its program. Preconceived stylistic allegiances were not allowed to undermine the strength and originality of their works, and consequently the students were able to offer designs of striking character.

Clockwise from top left:
Jacqueline Clawson, AIA
Weese Hickey Weese Architects, Ltd.

Thomas L. Shafer, AIA
Lohan Associates

Dennis E. Rupert, AIA
Hammond Beeby and Babka, Inc.

HONORABLE MENTION

The following have been selected for Honorable Mention:

A Cultural Exchange Center for Beijing
Chih-Yung Chiu
University of Michigan

Theinsville Historical Institute
Lee Lohman
University of Wisconsin-Milwaukee

BENN/JOHNCK AWARD

CA FIRST PLACE

**House for a Fellow of the
Skidmore Foundation of Architecture**

**Kurt Young Binter
University of Wisconsin - Milwaukee**

The task was to create a unique world, given a 25' by 125' lot surrounded by a 7 foot wall and a limited palette of materials. Inspiration and imagery for this project were drawn from assigned attributes and feelings: extroversion, winter, a plain, and the city of Anastasia, from Italo Calvino's Invisible Cities.
From the story two ideas were drawn: one of obsession, of being a slave to something; the other of Anastasia's resource of gems.
The tower is the place of labor. It contains a room for reading, writing, drawing, and contemplation. Its separation and proximity to the rudimentary dwelling allow the fellow to work at any time, and yet not live at the work place. The roof structure recalls Anastasia and her gemstones. Colored glass is held above the contemplation space much as a setting in a ring.
Sight lines and eye levels guide much of the design. An autonomous architectural expression was sought: in economy lies great strength.

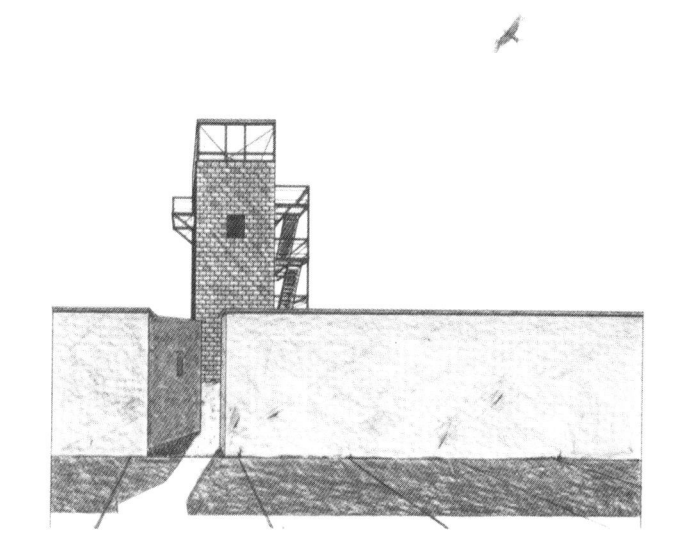

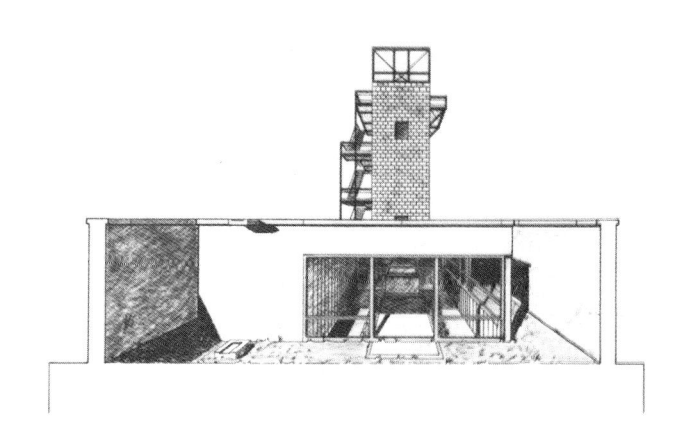

Jury Comments: "A simple yet compelling project... Very clever... Quietly gets the message across... well thought out, with a strong sense of emotion... really understood the program..."

SECOND PLACE CA

**SOM Foundation of Architecture
A Building in Chicago:
Meditations on the Idea of Enclosure**

**Alvyn Cheng-Chung Cheong
University of Wisconsin - Milwaukee**

On a small but extremely prominent Chicago site, a residence was developed for members of a Chicago architectural foundation. The ground floor has a gallery space for public viewing, direct street access, and a small preparation and storage area. On the second to ninth floors, fellows of the Institute are housed in single-floor residences or in duplexes. The tenth floor houses a community room, dining facilities, library, and roof deck and promenade. The concrete structure has projections extending to a maximum of 2.5 feet. Special attention was paid to the exterior wall and openings. Mechanical systems include radiant floor slabs, spacepak central air, and sprinklers. Internal spaces were developed first; then these ideas were translated into an exterior expression.

SECOND TO NINTH FLOOR - FELLOW RESIDENCE

Jury Comments: "Powerful, provocative idea...very strong presentation..."

Municipal Center and Park

Brian Peterson
University of Wisconsin - Milwaukee

In the village of Elm Grove, Wisconsin, on the western fringe of Milwaukee, a village hall constructed twenty years ago is now considered inadequate to accommodate expanded village services. The program consisted of remodeling the existing village hall and adding a library, police-fire station, assembly room, indoor swimming facility, and various recreational spaces. The park is ordered around two major spaces: a village green on the southeast corner containing major civic buildings and activities, and a circular athletic meadow surrounding a memorial grove and tower at the center. The two spaces are connected by a garden terrace and low wall which become the front facades of the pool house and village hall, integrating landscape and architecture. A road flows along the edge of the terrace, dividing the park into two worlds: a natural prairie and woodland on one side of the road and a more formal garden on the other.

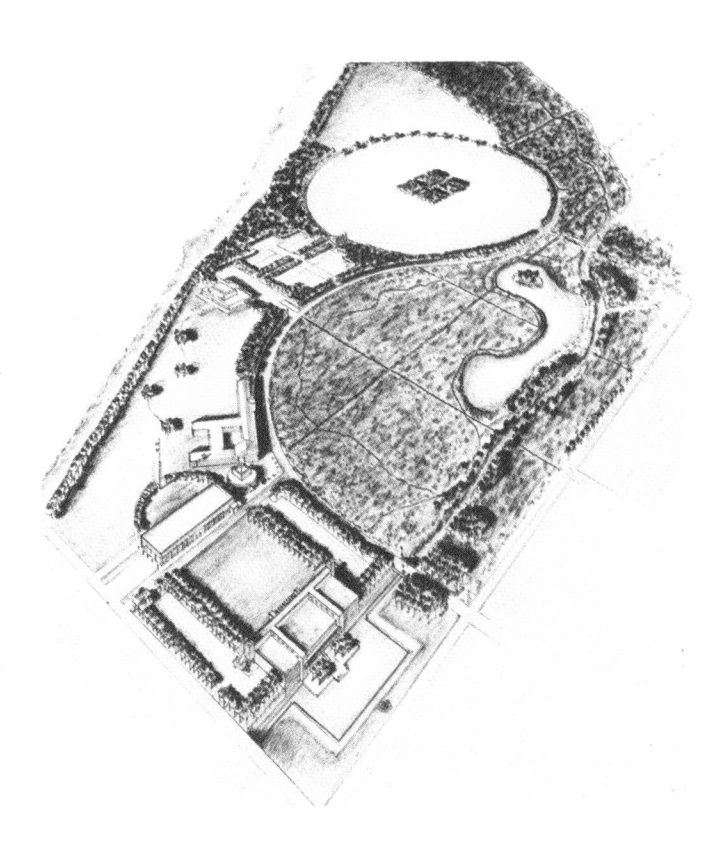

Jury Comments: "Beautiful drawings... excellent plan..."

ACKNOWLEDGEMENTS

DONORS

The Chicago Chapter of the American Institute of Architects wishes to acknowledge the following donors who have generously contributed to the programs of the Chapter during the year June 1, 1988-May 31, 1989:

AIA College of Fellows
Allright Parking
American Seating
Architecture and Law Committee of the Young Lawyers Section of the Chicago Bar Association
ASI Sign Systems
Bertrand Goldberg Associates
Binyon's
Butler Paper Company
Caboose Food and Liquors
Cagney + McDowell, Inc.
The Chicago Caterers
Chicago Dock and Canal Trust
Chicago Office of Fine Arts, Department of Cultural Affairs
Continental Woodworking Company
DeStefano/Goettsch, Ltd.
E. W. Corrigan Construction Company
Estate of Harold Dornbush
Euclid Insurance Agency
Fidninam (Chicago), Inc.
Fifield Development
Fine Arts Printing
First National Bank of Chicago
Foliage Design Systems
The Gettys Group, Inc.
Gilbane Building Company
Gleeson's
Graham Foundation for Advanced Studies in the Fine Arts
Graphics Support Services
Herman Miller, Inc.
Herner Geissler Woodworking Corporation
Huey Reprographics
IBI
Illinois Arts Council
Imperial Woodworking Company
Interface
Interior Woodworking Corporation
Jacobs Bros. Bagels
Jaymont Properties
The John Buck Company
Landrum & Brown
The Leather Center
Lego Systems, Inc.
Lincoln Property Company
McClier Corporation
Marciniak Photography
Master Typographers
Mellon Stuart Company
Metropolitan Structures
Miglin-Beitler Developments
Monday's
Moosehead
Moriama & Teshima Partners, Ltd., Toronto
Morse Diesel, Inc.
Mossner Printing Company
Nathan-D'Angelo, Ltd.
National Endowment for the Arts
Near North Reproductions
O'Malley and Company, Ltd., Events Marketing
Pepper Construction Company
Pickens Kane Moving and Storage
Printer's Row Restaurant
Printing Arts, Inc.
Prudential Plaza
R. Lawrence Kirkegaard & Associates
R. R. Donnelley & Sons Company
Robert Fugman and Associates Architects
Rosenzweig Professional Services Marketing
San Fratello's Speakeasy
Schal Associates
Sheet Metal Contractors Association; Chicago, Cook County and Lake Counties Chapter of SMACNA
Skidmore Owings and Merrill
Society of Architectural Administrators
South Loop Club
Steelcase/Stow & Davis
Stein and Company
The Swiss Grand Hotel
Thomas Design Systems
The Tile Foundation
Total Reproductions
Turner Construction Company
The Typesmiths, Inc.
U. S. Equities, Inc.
White Hen Pantry
Williams and Meyer
Women's Architectural League
The Woodward Agencies
Woodwork Corporation of America

1989 AWARDS PROGRAM COMMITTEE

Design Committee
Linda Searl, AIA, Chair
Anita R. Ambriz
Jon Barnes, AIA
Wallace Bowling, AIA
William Bradford, AIA
David Hansen, AIA
Paul Harding, AIA
Andrew Metter, AIA
Joseph Valerio, AIA

Interior Architecture Committee
Gregory W. Landahl, AIA, Chair
D. Scott O'Brien, Vice-Chair

Interior Awards Subcommittee
Nina Hancock, Chair
Patrick McConnell, Vice-Chair
Eileen Jones, Vice-Chair
Ann Uhlenhake
Barbara Pratt
Mark Kruse

Historic Resource Committee
Deborah Slaton, AIA, Chair
Harry J. Hunderman, AIA, Board Liaison
Tim Barton
William B. Coney, AIA
Carl Giegold
Gunny Harboe
Joseph Hoerner, AIA
Judith Hull
Stephen J. Kelley, AIA
Cheryl Kent
Anne McGuire
Dennis McFadden
Frank P. Michalski, AIA
Michael J. Pado, AIA
Tim Samuelson
Leslie Schwartz
Susan Tindall
Herman Wieland

1989 BOARD OF DIRECTORS

Steven F. Weiss, AIA
President

Sherwin Braun, AIA
First Vice-President

Leonard A. Peterson, AIA
Secretary

Thomas R. Samuels, AIA
Treasurer

John Syvertsen, AIA
Vice-President

Werner Sabo, AIA
Vice-President

John Tomassi, AIA
Vice-President

Harry Hunderman, AIA
Director

Anders Nereim, AIA
Director

John H. Nelson, AIA
Director

Tom Rossiter, AIA
Director

Linda Searl, AIA
Director

Yves Jeanty, AIA
Director

Frank Heitzman, AIA
Past President

Susan Dee
Associate Director

Paul Bodine
Associate Director

Kristine Fallon, AIA
Illinois Council Delegate

Robert Clough, AIA
Illinois Council Delegate

Jeffrey Conroy, FAIA
Illinois Council Delegate

James Zahn, AIA
Illinois Council Delegate

Ray Griskelis, AIA
Illinois Council Delegate

Robert Robicsek, AIA
Illinois Council Delegate

Lee Weintraub, AIA
Illinois Council Delegate

Geraldine McCabe-Miehle, AIA
Illinois Council Alternate

James Torvik, AIA
Illinois Council Alternate

Michael Youngman, AIA
Illinois Council Alternate

Kim Goluska
Professional Affiliate Director

Diane Bremen
SAA Liaison

Morgan Fleming
Student Director

Teresa Morelli
Student Director

Richard Cook, FAIA
Regional Director

Walter Lewis, FAIA
Regional Director

PROJECT TEAM

Anita R. Ambriz, Graphic Design
Jeanne Breslin, Computer Consultant
Catherine Weese, Editor
Peter Whitmer, Asst. Editor
Xpress Graphics, Postscript Typesetting
Walsworth Press Company, Printing